The Rag-Tag Team

A story of memories and magic in Michigan's Upper Peninsula

Bears Mark X

Bear's Story
penned by
Julie Hayes-Moe

Julie Hayes Moe

Tacoosh River Press

The Rag Tag Team

Julie Hayes-Moe

Tacoosh River Press
7848 Cole at Ackley
P.O. Box 398
Rapid River, MI 49878

Illustrated by Nikki McKenna

Library of Congress Catalog Card Number: 2001086817

ISBN: 0-9707343-0-1

Printed and bound in the United States of America.

Dedication

I dedicate this book to Gertrude Kathleen LaViolette Hayes, my mother, who gently led her children toward the light of education through constant exposure to literature. By helping with our homework, consistently encouraging us to read both the classics as well as contemporary works, combined with her firm rule "there'll be no trash in this house," she succeeded in installing in each of us a deep appreciation for education. For this I thank her.

I also dedicate this book to Lawrence Fredrick Hayes, my father. Although education was not one of his personal strengths, he clearly knew the value of an education and was totally dedicated to supporting and educating his children. For Daddy, college was a must for his kids. To do this and be able to spend time with his family were always his goals. Although often away from home, he spent most of his free time devising new and innovative ways to do just that. I thank him and I miss him.

WLH

Special Acknowledgements

Mary Ethel
Bill
Phyllis
Maggie
Peter
Mike

To my brothers and sisters for encouraging me to put on paper the dream of the dog run. Especially my brother Bill, who lovingly read and re-read and attempted to gently correct me. I also thank him for trying to persuade me on some of Bear's more lofty paragraphs... but he didn't succeed.

Thank you all for being terrific brothers and sisters through all our years.

JHM

In Memory of

Arne Grant Moe

9-24-32 to 1-15-01

A good man has passed into the
realm of precious memories
and is now 'Safely Home.'

As long as one remains
in memory—they remain
with us always.

Who knows…
perhaps we all have
a Shadow Team helping
us along the way.

JHM & Bear

CHAPTER 1

This is a tale—no pun intended—of loyalty, love, devotion, respect, family and friends. It's also a story of life and death, tragedy and heartbreak, past and present, memories and magic.

Animals communicate with one another all the time, but the legends say that on the eve of Christ's birth, animals have the power of speech. In addition, they are capable of activities and functions far beyond their normal and natural range. I for one know this is true. I experienced this phenomenon first hand. I am a dog. My name is Bear and the following events are true to the best of my recollection.

It was Christmas Eve, nineteen hundred and ninety eight. The fresh snow was a little damp and it clung to everything. The leafless trees and bushes were snow covered. Even the weeds and long grass held snow. The evergreens dipped gracefully under their load of white. The countryside was beautiful. The buildings and houses had a festive air. The snow created a picture-perfect, magical setting for the day. Our area is considered a winter wonderland to begin with, but this was special. There was an overwhelming feeling of excitement, a keen sense of great anticipation, almost a vibrancy in the air. Christmas Eve usually brings out the best, but I couldn't get over the feeling that some great event was about to happen; something... I don't know, perhaps spectacular is too strong, but something really great.

This would be the first Christmas in over 30 years that all of Old Mama's children, seven in all, and their families would be together under one roof for this, the most joyous of holidays. They agreed to meet at Bill's in Marquette. They had been together in the summers at camp on the occasions of Old Mama's special birthdays, seventy-five, eighty and eighty-five, but to be together for Christmas, words can barely describe their happiness.

Old Mama's children are not kids, but they are young at heart and when they gather together they seem to grow even younger. They remember well where they came from and where they've been. They also remember those they've loved that are gone. I am speaking especially of their Father. He's been gone as long as the last Christmas they spent together. They talk of him so much that I feel I know him, but that's not possible, for he's been gone longer than I, or any of my group can remember. I've often heard the old saying, "that as long as one lives in memory, one lives." I believe that.

Before going any further, let me tell a little about myself. As I said, my name is Bear and I am five and one-half years old. I am black with long guard hair that makes me look shaggy. My tail is quite large with long hair, always a nice feature for a dog I might add. My eyes are jet black and against my face sometimes you can't tell whether they're closed or open. Often I roll my eyes and a white ring appears around them, making me look critical, slighted or suspicious... whatever works. My father was a pedigreed Newfoundland and my mother was a magnificent German Shepherd. Therefore, weighing in at 100 pounds is not unusual.

My littermates and I were a mistake, definitely not planned. As a tribute to the people who owned my mother, a home was found for all eight of us. Eight big black puppies found homes. I was the first to go.

The couple that took me already had a monstrous standard poodle and a toy something or other. I really don't know why they wanted me. They were very very good to me, but it just didn't work with three vastly different dogs. I was there only four weeks when they called and wanted to return me. In the meantime, Julie had called looking for a puppy. All had been spoken for, however, arrangements were made for Julie and the couple to discuss the situation. On Thanksgiving Day a knock came on the door and there was Julie. She carried me to the car to meet Arne and Old Mama. It was a done deal. I had a new family. Old Mama held me in a soft blanket all the way home. It was decided I would keep my own name so I wouldn't be confused.

When I got to my new home, I met Stubby the cat. No tail, six toes on each paw and a disposition like a rattlesnake. We got along fine, she ignored me and I gave her wide berth. Stubby has a lovely daughter named Cubby. Cubby looks exactly like her name, she is a huge ball of black fur with a big puff of black where a tail should have been. Cubby has the most awesome eyes I've ever seen on any animal, they literally glow at times with golden, green facets. She's friendly and was very helpful in getting me settled into the household routine. On the other hand, every time I got within striking distance, Stubby would let me have a good slap. Stubby is the kind of cat that waits for unsuspecting dogs to run up to her and before they realize they've been had...they've been had.

Arne always refers to Stubby as his million-dollar cat.

Please bear with me—*Oops, another pun*—this won't take long to relate and it is a cute story. Seems one night when Stubby was just a kitten, Arne was doing some bookwork at the desk and had the safe open. The safe is much larger than the ordinary household type. Later that evening, Julie noticed the cat was missing and began to search and call. It was raining outside and several people had stopped by that evening, so out Julie went looking for the cat. NO CAT. Several times during the night Julie would go out and call for Stubby, but no show. Arne left the house early in the morning and Julie went into the utility room where the desk and safe were. She heard a faint meow. After calling a couple of times, Julie heard the cat again. Not being able to locate the exact source of the cry, Julie called Arne to come home and help look. Julie thought Stubby had gotten under the house. By the time Arne arrived the meowing had stopped. Fortunately Stubby loved Arne and would come when he called. Arne called her name and she cried out. Arne thought she was under the dryer. No, Julie had checked. "She's under the washer." No, it had also been checked. "She's under the house", Julie insisted. No, she can't be there, there's no way for her to get under there. Arne thought for a moment, walked over and began opening the safe. Julie said, "Forget that, it's not been opened for weeks." "Oh yes it has. I was in it last night." Arne said. He swung open the door and out walked Stubby no worse for the stay. They figured when the door closed Stubby thought well it's bedtime, guess I'll go to sleep. Being tiny, she didn't need a lot of breathing space. Plus, sleeping and not moving around she was okay. A happy ending to something that could have been tragic.

Prior to my arrival in Julie's life she had a West Highland terrier for ten years. Her cousin, Betty Ann, had given Peppi to her and the little dog lived to be 18 years old. Before Peppi there was Jennie the Bassett. Jennie was a real terror. Her name should have been "Trouble" from the stories I've heard about her. They both were well loved and sadly missed. Stories are still told of them. Enough about them, back to my story.

Wait! Wait! I must tell one story about Jennie that I personally think is hilarious. It seems that Julie and a friend were going fishing very early one morning at a campground. Before they launched the boat, Jennie was let out of the truck to give her a little run and some potty time before getting into the boat. The launch was far enough away from campers and there didn't appear to be too many of them around anyway. Well, Jennie didn't return and after a couple of whistles and calls, Julie started out looking. Down the path she went, finally coming upon a man with no shoes on, his hands on his hips, staring at the point where two small inland lakes connect. "Excuse me." Julie said, "Good morning. Have you seen my dumb dog?" He turned and fixed Julie with an icy stare. "If you mean that gigantic Basset Hound, yes, and it's far from dumb. That damn dog pushed up the zipper of our tent, then licked my wife in the face, who woke up screaming. When I tried to get it out, it grabbed my wife's bra and ran with it. I chased it. It ran out in the water. See!"

Oh Boy! There was Jennie out on a small sand bar trying to shake loose the bra that was caught on her lower fangs. Julie waded out in the water to her waist to get to the sand bar. After retrieving the bra (that was really no worse for the wear) Julie offered to pay damages. By this time, the braless lady was out of the tent and a few more campers had wandered down to the shore. A good laugh was had by all.

CHAPTER 2

Earlier that Christmas Eve afternoon as my family, Julie, Arne, Smoke and I headed for Marquette from Munising, we were watching the big lake.

We were around Sand River when we noticed a big self unloader, (Great Lakes freighter), slowly making its way toward Marquette. Julie remarked that everyone on that boat has a family and most will be separated for Christmas day. When she didn't talk for awhile, I knew she was deep in thought about Christmas days from long ago.

Sometime later, when everyone had arrived at the place of great happiness and festivities, the freighter began turning into the lower harbor toward the power plant. Nothing much was said; words were unnecessary, everyone had similar thoughts. All the while it approached, one or two of the group stood watch by the big windows. Still others took turns at the big telescope set up at one end of the living room. The boom on the freighter was all lit up with white lights. The forward searchlight was slowly moving back and forth in front of the ship. The big light slid easily across the black water almost in a greeting, a greeting from the past, a voice long dead saying, "I love you all. Merry Christmas dear family. I am with you in spirit."

The Dad had sailed the Great Lakes for over 20 years and most of those years on self unloaders very close in size to the one approaching. I said earlier that I knew this was going to be a very memorable night.

The family was upstairs and we were in the den downstairs. Our human folks (I refuse to call them owners) take us everywhere. That means we'd better be good and we'd better be quiet.

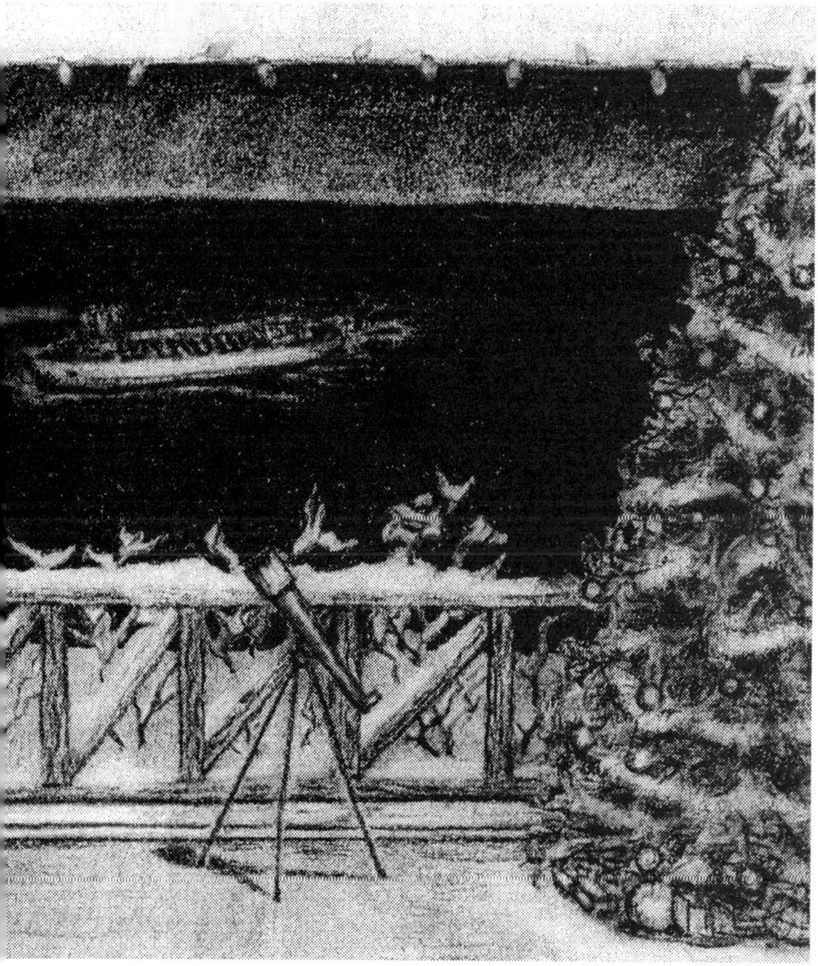

When we are all together we number nine, counting Old Mama's dog it would be ten, but she wasn't with us tonight. She doesn't mix well with noisy people and prolonged activity. If she's not with Old Mama, she's with Julie or left alone for a few hours of time by herself. The warmth in the room was as much a feeling of the season and a sense of camaraderie among the occupants as from the fireplace. The group knows one another fairly well and are comfortable with each other.

The fire was burning slowly in the waning hours of its life. In the soft glow of the quiet flames one could barely make out the figures sprawled unceremoniously around the room. Christmas music drifted down the open stairway and the muffled sounds of voices and activity upstairs could be heard but not to the point of distraction.

The big stone fireplace with its wide hearth was the focal point of the room. A huge brass ship's compass sat on one end of the hearth. The other end a plump plaid pillow, Buddy's bed.

The room was comfortable with many big windows and a set of glass doors leading to a small deck. The furniture looked great and very comfortable, but none of the group would be so rude as to settle themselves on any of it. The deck lights cast shadows on the trees and snow adding to the warmth and glow of the room.

CHAPTER 3

Looking about, I placed them all in my mind. There's Buddy, Ben, Buck, Deacon, Dakota, Misty, Shannon, Smoky, and of course, myself. We'd all been fed, watered and had a turn outside.

Thus, we were lounging and dozing. Most of us half a sleep. Buddy jumps from his pillow on the hearth—his people own the house—and stands directly in front of the fire. His little frame throws huge shadows that wiggle around the walls and make strange looking silhouettes. He suggests we play games, quiet ones, of course. Let's get to know each other better. Deacon slowly raised his head, fixed Buddy with a scowling stare, "Are you crazy or what? I just rode 300 miles and I don't want to play games. No offense please, but gimme a break." "300 miles, I came 600 miles," said Buck. Misty, the oldest of the group, suggested that distance didn't really matter, but getting along with each other is the most important thing. "However," she added, "if anyone is counting miles, my family and I moved 800 miles from Oklahoma to Green Bay this summer. That's if anyone is interested in miles." Ever the host with the most, Buddy, persisted in trying to get everyone's attention and involvement in socializing. A shift in position, a roll of an eye or a low *harrump* was the only answer he got.

A log had burned in half and fell with a thud and shower of sparks. Smoky jumped to his feet, barking, then started to shake uncontrollably. Ben yelled, "What's with him?" "Stop it! Leave him alone and don't make fun," I said. "He's my brother. None of you understand what he has been through. Get over here, Smoke, and lay down by me." With his ears flat against his head and his tail down, Smoky moved over next to me. He whispered, "I'm sorry, Bear. I couldn't help it. Did I embarrass you?" "No kid, it's okay. Lay down and take a little nap." "I can't. Now they all think I am weird." Smoky said. "Oh hush, it's okay. Don't worry," I replied. He laid down next to me and curled up. He opened and closed his eyes a couple of time, but soon drifted off into a gentle sleep.

The room was quiet again with only an occasional snore or running and jerking like dogs do when they sleep. People are right when they see us running in our sleep and say we're dreaming and chasing rabbits. Sometimes it's not dreams, but nightmares that make us run.

I couldn't drift off as quickly as Smoky. I thought about him and wondered if he would ever completely get over the accident. Would he ever get use to noises and not be so skittish and jumpy. He'd come along way since that terrible day when his dear friend, John, was killed in a highway accident. Smoky was riding in the front seat of the pickup with John when they hit a semi. The passenger air bag saved Smoky. He wasn't hurt with cuts and bruises, but his spirit and memory were marked deeply.

Smoky was a pound puppy and John got him when he was a couple of months old. Per usual, people who love their dogs will get a new friend if something happens to their old one. Smoky replaced "Buck", a big golden retriever, that at 15 years old suffered a stroke and had to be put down. Arne and Julie adopted Smoky after the accident. You see, John was Arne's younger brother.

Smoky is a handsome black and white, mostly English Setter and Border Collie, with a wonderful long, flowing tail and a large wide forehead. His nose is freckled as are his feet and legs. He often stands with his toes pointed out and it makes him look silly. His big brown eyes hold lots of sorrow, but he's still young and has tons of energy. He loves to play with anyone and anything. He loves the outdoors and he especially enjoys chasing the birds from the bird feeders. When the birds are feeding heavily, Smoky has to be in the dog run behind the house. Smoky, you're a survivor. You'll make it just fine.

Chapter 4

Taking a look around the room,
I thought about the others.
Little Buddy, never aware of his
size because of his confidence and
big heart. Buddy's a pure bred.
What can be said after that?
Except, he's an all around
great little guy.

A small brown Dachshund that some students couldn't care for anymore. Thus, he was adopted by Bill and Anita. Buddy went from a small student apartment to a big house on a hill over looking the lower harbor. The house has a deck across the front and as Buddy strolls the deck he thinks there is nothing he can't do. In reality, I believe it's the height and the vista, but who knows. Buddy followed Max, a little black and brown

Dachshund that Bill and Anita had for over ten years. Max had an inoperable tumor on his spine and suffered greatly. With heavy heart and much sadness they decided to have him put to sleep. Buddy's loved and he knows it.

Laying tightly curled, closest to the fire, is Misty. The Klines are her people. At 14 years old, Misty is the oldest of the group. She is a mixed breed that runs heavily to Border Collie in size and looks. Misty is a lovely tan and white with soft long hair and deep warm eyes with lashes that would be the envy of any lady. Misty and her littermate wandered into the Kline's yard when they were about 10 weeks old. The Kline kids had been waiting to get a Bassett, but when a home was quickly found for Misty's brother, that did it. They decided they wanted to keep her. No Bassett, they were told, if she stays. "We want to keep her. We want to keep her.", they cried. Lucky lady Misty. Misty is gentle, quiet and very wise. I don't know whether it's her nature or just her years. Misty replaced Kiko, a big Malamute. Kiko lived with the Klines for many years in Gallup, New Mexico. When a move to Oklahoma was decided, the vet suggested against her going because of health problems. The vet knew a lady who wanted a dog like Kiko. Thus, it was determined she would remain in Gallup. The lady who got her would always let Kiko ride in the front seat. When in town if they passed by Long John Silvers, a fish place, Kiko would have lunch, a fish sandwich without mayo.

Off to the side of the room with their legs stuck straight out in front of their bodies lay Shannon and Dakota.

Those two dogs can take up more room than any five dogs. Shannon is a large brown beauty with dark brown eyes. One good looking Labrador. She's solid and carries herself well. She's a few weeks older than I am. She had one litter of pups and Dakota is from that litter. When Shannon had her pups she taught them to be independent from early on. She would nurse them, cover them with a blanket and march upstairs to be with Mary and Kirk.

Dakota is a big yellow Labrador. Her nose is mauve colored (that's pink in regular language). Dakota always looks like she's frowning or worried. She could be a poster dog for her breed. She may be picture-perfect, but she has one big hang up for a Lab, she hates water. Water of any sort, except to drink. Bathing her is a struggle and swimming is out of the question. Shannon and Dakota dote on Sean and Little Kirk, the grand kids. The dogs love going to camp. Shannon to swim and Dakota to lay in the dirt and shade. Shannon replaced another Shannon. The first Shannon was a fanciful, wild and woolly Irish Setter. She ran away every single chance she got. Now, *there* was a dog! Every year she produced a litter of puppies, with litters ranging from 10 to 13, she never lost one. The last year she was bred, however, she had only one, great big, male puppy. The last hurrah. No more. This Shannon was 15 years old when she died.

Only because I know where he is, can I distinguish Ben laying by the window at the foot of the stairs. Black as the night, Ben is huge, gentle and beautiful. Not unlike myself, I might add. He has a fine large head with very expressive eyes. Ben's eyes are sort of an amber or bronze color. He is part Golden Retriever and Newfoundland, a real beauty. What a dickens. Phyllis was worried whether Ben would ever grow up. He was almost classified as incorrigible and could have ended up returning to the humane society down state. He was lucky; Phyllis and Little Mary had fallen head over tails in love with him. This Ben replaced a very similar Ben that was stolen from their fenced in back yard one fall at the beginning of hunting season.

The Bens followed Schooner and Ceasar, big German Shepherds. Schooner chewed rocks and wore her teeth down. No matter what they did she would find a rock and chew it. Even with her teeth worn to nubs, she lived 13 years.

Ceasar had been horribly mistreated. She was beaten and shot with a pellet gun. Chained outside most days without food or water was her life. She was taken to the humane society in the Sault and Phyllis adopted her. She was a loving and loyal friend for 12 years.

Right in the middle of the room, with front paws stretched directly out in front, laying on his belly with head flat on his fore legs is Deacon. Staring into the flames with eyelids half closed probably recalling some glorious hunting adventure he had with his boys. Deacon is sleek and shiny, a dark chocolate color and a build that shows excellent blood lines. The muscles in his shoulders and rump are very apparent. Deacon's a working Labrador. He loves the cold black waters of a lake or bay. In the fall the dry reeds and grasses along the waters edge whisper to him, "let's hunt", "mark", "dead bird". With the ducks and geese winging over head, and the sounds of the shotguns, he's at work and loving every minute of it. He's tough. Yeah, he's tough. He had to be tough; he was raised with four boys. The boys are Peter and Merrylie's. Deacon is seven years old.

He almost died as a puppy. He had Parvo and spent many, many days in the animal hospital. Larry would go visit him each day and take him a stuffed toy or something from home. The boys paid the vet and hospital bill by selling their snowmobile. The vet said love and tender care pulled him through as much as the medicine. For months he looked like a starving waif. His skin hung on his frame and you could count his ribs. The vet said that Deacon contracted the illness between shots. Perhaps at a highway rest area.

Deacon replaced Levi, a giant dog. A most wonderful Yellow Labrador with a head that looked like it was sculpted. Levi was also a working Labrador and dear friend to the boys. He was killed instantly by a very reckless driver. His boys made it safely across the street, but Levi wasn't so lucky.

I have to relate a short story about how Levi embarrassed Pete on a hunting outing with Pete's boss. Seems Peter's boss had spent many hours building a duck blind that looked like a big round bale of hay. It had a wooden frame covered in chicken wire. The outside, of course, was hay, painstakingly threaded through the wire. One end had an opening for the door, the other end had a lift section that raised for shooting and hid the gun barrels. Levi had trained for days on end. He knew his routine perfectly. When Pete, or anyone shot, he was given the command "mark" if more than one bird was down or "dead bird" if only one was down. With the command Levi was to leave the blind via the door. Not so on the hunt with the boss. The command was given and boom, Levi exploded out the front of the blind, completely destroying it, leaving the wonderful creation in shambles around Peter and his boss. As Peter and his boss crawled out of the mess, Levi laid the last of the ducks in front of them.

Buck got up, shook himself a little and ambled over just as I was going to tell about him. He'd been laying smack up against the patio doors because it was the coolest place in the room. Buck is a real class act, one good looking dog. He's the kind that with one look you know he has all the right papers. He's an Alaskan Malamute. Heavy gray fur with black tips, snow white legs, chest and muzzle and the tell tale black "V" on his forehead. What a beauty. He's only about six or seven months old, but weighs over 75 pounds. I remember seeing him at about 10 weeks old. He was a big ball of white fluff with teeth like little needles. He wanted to play, but I was napping, so Buck bit me on the foreleg. I snapped at him good and loud. He got the message. He's the youngest of our group but he's smart as a whip and very well behaved. Buck talks. Well, not like tonight when we can talk. But he has a tremendous range of sound that he makes. It appears he is really trying to talk. While making these sounds he shakes his head and paws the carpet with his feet. Buck is a very unique dog.

He is a little shy around us yet because of the reason he came to be Mike's dog. The story is still pretty fresh in our minds. You see Buck replaced Tabers. Tabers was a glorious looking huge Yellow Labrador. He had one goal in life, to protect and love his family. The family in turn loved him dearly. Tabers and Jake grew up together. They spent hours rolling around on the floor and would often fall asleep draped over one another. Tabers was a great watchdog and sounded an alarm if anything was going on outside the house.

Now to get back to the story. It seems that Kathy and the kids, Jake and Lauren had been on a short vacation. When arriving home Jake ran to the bedroom where his dad, Mike, was sleeping. Tabers was also asleep on the foot of the bed. When Jake reached the side of the bed, Tabers was either startled or confused, but whatever, he bit Jake on the arm. It was a terrible bite. Closing the wound took many stitches. In that split second everything changed. Tabers made a fatal mistake. He couldn't be trusted again. He had to be put down. The sorrow that descended on the whole family was heart breaking. Everyone cried. When they called the rest of the family to relay the awful news, the whole family grieved with them. It was a very, very sad time.

"Bear, what are you doing?" Buck asked, "Why are you sitting up watching all of us?" "Oh, I was just thinking how different we all are and yet how much alike in so many ways we are." I replied. "You know each of us has a story to tell. We're quite a bunch when all together." "Where's Abby? Old Mama's dog", Buck asked. "Why isn't she here?"

"You know my Mike found her when he was hunting birds in a cornfield in Iowa. She was covered with a thin coat of ice, curled in a tight ball. Actually she was freezing to death. Mike picked her up and put her in his jacket and took her to a vet. It was touch and go for a few hours, but she came around."

Abby is a small dog by our standards. She stands about 20 inches high and is mostly white with big blackish spots. Her hair is short and wiry. She has one motley eye and it often gives her a crazy look. She bites her toenails and so does Smoky. What a sight. There they are, holding a leg up and trying to get in the proper position. You can hear them crunching and snapping. Unbelievable.

Buddy had been walking around the room. Stopping and saying a few words to each one. They were now mostly awake and listening.

"Is she really as bad as they say?" Ben turned toward Deacon for an answer. Deacon replied, "Well, whenever I've been to Old Mama's she treated me good." It's probably your size." Misty said. "No." I interjected. "Abby's not afraid of anything. I think she'd tackle a Mountain Lion if it was after her food." "Well,

I've never met her, but I've heard good things about her. I know she's a terrific little watch dog." Misty added. "She was hit by a car on Labor Day a year and a half ago." Shannon said, "If I remember correctly."

"Yes she was. I saw the whole thing, and I can tell you it was a sight I don't want to see repeated. It was horrible. She can be a wild one. When she would get free, she would run crazy. Never looking, just running back and forth. No point, just run. The vet said she exhibits behavior that shows she had been abused. If someone makes a quick move toward her, she often crouches, drops to the floor and usually piddles all over. She sometimes trembles and shakes like she is having a seizure and then she wants to be held.

It was toward evening. She broke free from Old Mama, who was hooking her to the tie out. Abby ran head long down the driveway into the road and smack into a van. The impact threw her into the ditch on the far side of the road. I thought she was a goner. The van stopped and we all ran to her. But, before we could get there, she staggered out of the ditch into the road and collapsed. That's it, I thought. Poor little Abby, what an end for her when she was just beginning to trust and enjoy life. Julie got to her and knelt next to her stroking her head and gently calling her name. Abby opened her eyes, but the spark was gone and she was bleeding from a badly cut front shoulder. Julie and another woman eased Abby on a folded blanket and put her in the back seat of the car. Old Mama got in the back and talked to her and patted her softly. Julie called the vet's office.

They headed for Harvey, to the Marquette Animal Clinic. The vet, Dr. Swanson, had come into his office for another emergency, so he was waiting for them. The doctor examined her very carefully, but made no promises. He said he would give her medicine, have her stay the night and do some x-rays. Old Mama called first thing in the morning. Abby was alive, but no x-rays had been done. They said they'd call us later in the day. Dr. Swanson called at 3:30 p.m. and said we could come get her, but she would need some tender loving care for sometime and she would have to take some medicine for infection for a couple of weeks. Time would tell. In the waiting room, Dr. Swanson cautioned them to watch for bladder problems because of the accident. With that, Abby promptly peed about a pint all over the floor. Dr. Swanson laughed, 'Well, so much for that area of concern.' Poor Abby was in so much pain. She would cry and whimper when she had to move. Gradually, she regained her strength, but it took months for the big cut on her shoulder to heal. There still isn't any hair on parts of the scar and it often bothers her yet. Old Mama puts lotion on it to keep it soft. Well, I didn't mean to go on so long about the accident, but I guess there's a lesson for all of us in telling it."

CHAPTER 5

"It's kind of sad that she can't be with us." said Dakota. "Everyone else is here."

"I know why she's not here." Smirked Shannon. "Because of Little Kirk. He's small. If he would grab at her or startle her, who knows what she might do. She's not to be trusted."

"It's really hard to believe she's such a terror.", replied Buck. "When I was there she was pretty good."

"I think she's a lot of fun." Smoky said, hesitantly looking around the room. "The only time she really gets wild or noisy is if someone comes by the house or you try and take her food."

"That covers a lot of time, Sport." Deacon commented. "If she gets nutty when anyone comes around, it's best to keep an eye on her."

Just then Buddy jumped up on the hearth and began running back and forth. Let's go get her! Let's go get her!

"Have you slipped a cog or something?" Ben asked. "What are you talking about?"

"Yes." Buck said. "It might be nice to have her here."

"Give me a break. Who's going to drive the car?" laughed Dakota.

Everyone started to laugh.

"No", Buddy yelled. "I'm serious. Let's go get her!"

"And just how do you propose to do that?" Shannon cracked. "Take a cab?"

By this time, all were howling with laughter and rolling around on the floor. The one liners were whipped around and everyone had at least one smart remark. Buddy gave a sharp bark to get everyone's attention. "I'm very serious." he said. "Let's go get her!"

"Okay, okay!" I said. "It would be nice to have her with us. They're all upstairs and we're all down here. It would be great, but it's out of the question."

"No it's not." Buddy chimed. "I have a plan. It hit me all at once while we were talking about her. We can do it but it will take every one of us. All or none."

"What are you talking about little friend?" asked Ben. "Maybe I missed something."

"Buck have you ever heard about dog teams?" questioned Buddy. "You know what I mean... sled dogs. It's your heritage, it's your breed, your nature."

"Yes." Buck replied. "But, what does a dog sled have to do with this?"

"Everything." Buddy yipped. "Everything! That's my plan. It can be done, I know it can."

"Do you think so Buddy? Do you really think so?" Poor Smoky always trusting and believing everything.

"Smoke, sit down. It's not gonna work cause it's just a pipe dream. Come back over here little brother. Don't get too excited." I said.

"Hey, little guy! Get off that hearth. The heat is boiling your brain." Laughed Ben.

"Listen Sport." Deacon soothed. "We'd all like to see Abby here, but certain things can't be done even by the best of us."

"No!" Buddy replied. "At least listen to me."
"I have a feeling if we don't, we'll be up the rest of the night listening." Groaned Shannon. "Go for it."

"He's the host, so give him his say or we won't hear the end of it." Misty said. "Remember what they say about the best presents coming in small packages. Well, perhaps the best story will come from the littlest dog. No offense meant." Misty added.

"Calm down everyone. Give Buddy a chance to tell his plan or I'll side with him for playing games." I thought I'd toss that in for the fun of it, since the last thing I wanted to do was play games. However, it quieted the group and after a couple of minutes everyone was politely waiting for "the plan".

"Well," Buddy began, "Did you ever hear of the Iditarod?"

Only blank looks answered the question.

"Well, how about the U.P. 200 or the Midnight Run?" Buddy continued.

Not a flicker of recognition crossed a muzzle. So I replied, "I have indeed heard about them. In fact, I saw some of the teams when they crossed the road at Ackerman Lake on M-94. I also saw teams resting in Rapid River before they headed across the Bays de Noc to Escanaba."

Buddy persisted, "Come on you guys, surely you know what I'm talking about."

"Well," said Shannon, "Dakota and I were in the family room when Sean watched a show on TV about some sled dogs. Frankly, I fell asleep and barely remember anything. Dakota, do you remember seeing that show?"

"Yes, I do." Dakota said, "When a team of dogs and sleigh went through the ice, I couldn't bear to watch anymore. So I went and laid down in the foyer."

"Buck," Buddy started, "You, of all of us, must know something about sled dogs. It's your breed, your heritage."

"Yes, yes," Buck answered, slightly annoyed at being put on the spot, so to speak. "There are sled dogs on my family tree. We're noted for our strength and endurance. We're the work force, the transporters. I'm proud of my heritage, but I am not a sled dog. I've had no training. I am a friend and a companion to my Mike and family and I won't apologize for that."

"Where's this all heading anyway?" asked Ben. "I am getting real uneasy."

"It's heading to Rapid River to get Abby. That's where it's heading", squealed Buddy, his voice raising to a squeak. "That's my plan. We're going to form a sled team, grab a sleigh and head to Rapid by way of the abandoned railroad grades."

"Hold it! Hold it! Hold it!" Deacon got up from his spot in the middle of the room. "A bunch of lap dogs we're not, but we're not sled dogs either. Now ease up little guy." With that he stretched and dropped with a soft thud back on the floor. Subject closed... or so he thought.

CHAPTER 6

Knowing Buddy, the skirmish may have been over, but the war hadn't even begun.

Everyone was very quiet and I felt it was time for me to step in with some common sense and peace making.

"Sled dogs are bred and born for the lifestyle they have. They're wonderful to watch. They're trained and tested for the pull and the run. They're very good at what they do. These sled dogs and the trainers or owners practice almost year round. Buddy, we are not sled dogs!"

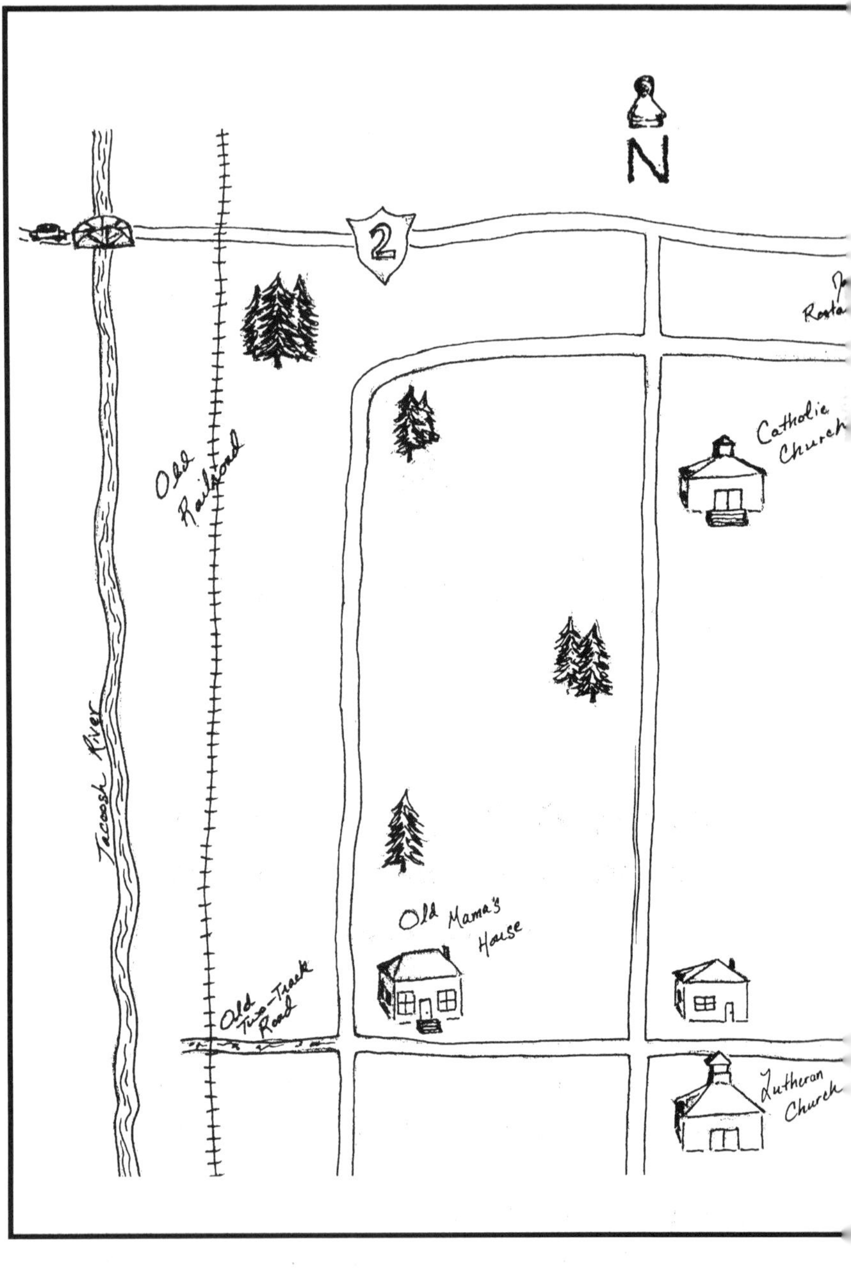

Misty spoke quietly, "Buddy, ideas like the one you're suggesting take years of planning, training and organization. It can't be done."

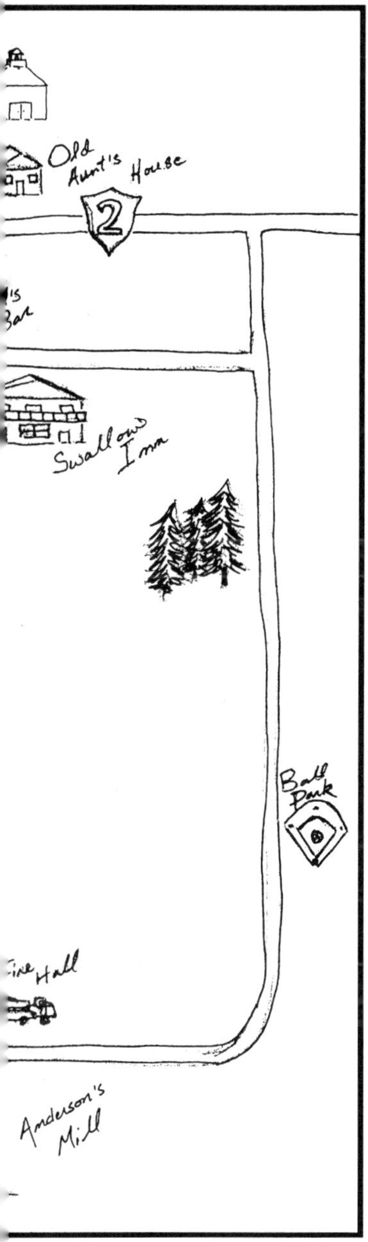

Again, the room grew quiet and we could hear the muffled voices from upstairs. Buddy walked slowly back and forth on the hearth. Finally, he said, "Can I at least finish telling you my plan and after I give you the details, then have you decide?" We all nodded in polite agreement.

"Bear, what goes right by Old Mama's house north to south?"

"The river." I answered, not really paying attention.

"No! The old Soo line railroad. It's been abandoned for years." Buddy corrected.

"Oh ya, that's right. It goes all the way to Eben. Right past Arne's grandmother's farm." I replied.

"That's right." Buddy continued, "By using a couple of old roads we can connect with another abandoned railroad that goes through Deerton and Sand River. My

Anita has told me stories about that area and we've gone for lots of rides on the old roads. That railroad comes right into Marquette. It passes directly below my backyard down by the lakeshore. See, a direct line from this spot to Old Mama's."

"You're crazy!" Shannon squealed. "I don't know why I wasted time listening. I could have been napping."

"You're nuttier than a can of peanuts." laughed Dakota.

"Now Dakota, don't get personal." Shannon chided.

Smoky stood up quickly. "Bear, is Buddy crazy?" "Is he?"

Poor Smoky, always so worried. I looked at him and nodded for him to stay close by. "Take it easy kid. Don't get so worked up. There are things that can be done and there are things that can't. Often even when you know something won't work, or can't be done, it's fun to talk about it. It's like, you know, exercising your imagination."

CHAPTER 7

I turned back to the group. I felt I had to play the devil's advocate. (Pretty good term for a dog, eh?) "There isn't anyone who enjoys the cold, wind and snow, like I do.

There is nothing like laying curled in a tight ball with your face tucked down and your tail fanned around your head. The wind pelting you with snow and packing it in all around you. I love laying there thinking about life in general. Day dreaming, remembering special times or sometimes my mind is simply blank. Then all of a sudden I get the urge to take a good run. I get up, shake the snow from my coat and head out across the orchard, down into the old sandpit, up the hill to the woods and on to the swamp. The snow can be chest deep, but I plod on. It feels great. My heart thumps and my breath makes icicles of my whiskers. After a while I come dragging back with great balls of snow clinging to my feet and my long belly fur. The very best part of it all is when I stand by the door and give a short bark. It opens with a friendly welcome to a warm room. I hope you folks are listening."

Buddy gave two loud barks. He yelled, "Hey, you said you'd listen to me."

"I know little friend and we will. Go ahead with your plan."

The room was alive with whispered conversations. A groan here and there, a laugh or two. "Hush everyone. I know I get a little long-winded at times, but we agreed to let Buddy give us the details of his plan. Continue Buddy." The drone in the room had gone down a level or two, but was far from quiet. "Hush." I said again. Only this time I added a small low growl just for emphasis. It worked. All became silent and although I noted a few bored looks, I sensed everyone was primed for the rest of "the plan".

"I am not asking you to do what these professional working dogs do. I'm only saying we can at least try. If we can't do it, we can come back and no one will be the wiser. But, we'd know we tried. I have the outline of the route and I know it very well." Buddy went on, "But, we need harnesses, some warm robes for the sleigh and of course a sleigh. I have everything we need including the sleigh. The sleigh isn't right here, but it's down by the railroad."

Misty spoke up, "Buddy, there is no way I could make such a trip. I am too old and I've always lived in areas with less snow and cold." "Don't worry Misty. I've thought of that also. You'll ride with me on the sleigh." "Oh sure, you and Misty will ride." Shannon cracked, "and we'll run. Well, I..." "Shannon, let him finish. Please, just listen."

"The stuff for the harnesses is in the garage along with a sheep skin and some wool blankets for the sleigh. The sleigh itself doesn't belong to us, it belongs to a fisherman down below the hill. It's been leaning along side a building for a couple of weeks now. I saw it only yesterday." Buddy was on a roll. He went on like he had his right mind. "Misty will ride with me and I will be..." he hesitated and looked around, "the driver." I'd be happy to run, but with these legs of mine, it's out of the question. The teams or partners would be "The browns", Deacon and Shannon, then "the blacks", Bear and Ben, the "the kids", Smoky and Dakota, and finally, our very own "Buck" as the lead. The room fell absolutely silent. Each one thinking their own thoughts, each one dreaming their dreams, each one wondering, "Is it possible? Could we pull it off?"

It's wild. It's crazy. It's not sensible. It's not practical. It's asking for trouble. It's dangerous. It's foolishness.

No one made a sound. No one said a word, waiting for someone else to start. No one wanted to be the first to say "yes" or "no". What a tremendous adventure. What a terrible disaster. Could it work? Could we do it? It sounded so simple, so easy.

I was surprised when I heard a voice. My own. I couldn't believe I was taking this seriously. I said, "The teams are placed wrong. Ben and I are strongest in the pull. We should be nearest the sleigh. I'll be on the left because my right leg is weaker. I sprained it once. Put Smoke and Shannon next with Smoke on the right. So if he gets scared he can turn and see me. Shannon, being older, will help keep him calm. Next, of course, you'd have Deacon and Dakota. They have strength and speed. Then Buck would be in the lead. If Buck wouldn't work out as the lead, Deacon would be the natural replacement." Good heavens. I couldn't believe what I was saying. It must be the heat, for the room felt like it was getting warmer.

The room remained quiet. The fire was still burning with a cheery blaze flashing here and there along the remains of the criss crossed logs. The silence remained, but a feeling of energy, of power, of magic was beginning to settle on the occupants. Something was happening. The old memories were stirring. The days, the years, perhaps even the centuries were being peeled away.

Chapter 8

"Let's do it." Yelled Deacon. Almost simultaneously Ben shouted, "I'm for it!" With that, everyone was talking at once. The die was cast!

Buddy was beside himself with excitement. "Yes, yes. We'll do it. We will, I know we will." "Wait!" I hollered, "Wait, think! Think what we're discussing. This is not a lark. It won't be a game. We're not talking about running around the neighborhood two or three times and coming back to this warm cozy room. Think what he's suggesting. Use your heads for something besides sniffing the next dog you meet." That was a crude remark. However, I needed these furry four legged beasts to use the natural intellect their creator gave them to save them from themselves. Again, the room fell silent. Unable to stop my thoughts, my mind once again began to race with ridiculous thoughts. Fantastic images fell into place. My imagination was on the fast track. I'm not in such bad shape. I run every morning and night from the house to the swamp. Up hills, down hills through the brush, up and over fallen trees. I do it fast so Julie doesn't know how far I go. Although, I did once hear the man up the road tell her he saw me in the woods behind his house.

Ben, he's in good shape. He runs each day with Phyllis and she runs several miles a day. Deacon is great., he keeps in shape following the boys, chasing behind motor bikes and four wheelers. He swims almost daily in the pond.

Smoky, Dakota and Buck have youth on their side. Tell them it's fun and they'll do anything. Shannon isn't in what you'd call racing form, but I think she'd do her part just fine.

Stop it! Stop it! I silently yelled to myself. Don't get caught up in this madness... and it is madness. Again, my mind took off on a tangent. I knew the railroad grades Buddy was referring to and the back roads. I couldn't stop thinking about this crazy plan of his. In my mind I ran the route by myself. Stop it you fool. Just stop it! Before complete insanity takes over.

I was brought back to reality by the sound of Deacon and Buck talking together in low tones. "You know,

Sport, I think we could pull this off. What do you think?" "Well, what bothers me most is none of us have ever been in a harness or rigged up like a team of any kind. It's not like we'd be pulling anything real heavy." Deacon added. "The sleigh and the three small dogs... I could pull myself and I'm sure you could too." "Hey, fellas listen to what you're talking about. Think for a minute. I know you're both bored and just itching to get outside and run for a bit, but for heavens sake, put some thought into this." All of a sudden I noticed everyone had moved in closer and were listening to our conversation. Buddy started in again. He had stopped being the host with the most, and was, in my opinion, fast becoming a real agitator. "We can do it, I know we can. We are not a bunch of pampered show dogs who spend their lives preening for the next show. We're down to earth ordinary garden-variety dogs and we're free. Free to think what we want. Free to dream, free to soar, free to take to the open road."

"Oh, cut the crap." Shannon said. "We're ready to do it. You sound like a politician." "By the way," Misty cut in, "there is absolutely nothing wrong with show dogs. They are the crem de la crem of each breed and in a way, they make us all look good. Just remember they were chosen by people who love them just as we were chosen by our folks who love us."

"Are we, or aren't we going to rise to the challenge?" Shannon whined. "Because I'm ready to go if we are." "Shannon, for crying out loud, think what you're saying," I said. "This is nuts for us to go off half cocked into the night like we had our right minds." I looked around the room. The looks I got back told me I had lost the argument. I stood up and slowly circled the group. In my heart of hearts I was secretly proud of them. Each of them, for reasons, known only to themselves, wanted to do this. It wasn't just about Abby. The desire came from deep within their hearts and spirits. A remnant of a long dead heritage. No matter what we look like now, we all came from the same ancestors many ages ago.

"Well Buddy, it looks like we're ready to put your "plan" into action. What's next?" I asked. To my surprise, the group became all business. Buddy was like a tin toy that someone had wound up. He jumped up and ran across the hearth. He leaped from the hearth to the couch and onto a big chair then stopped. "I knew you'd agree! Let's get started my friends. We have much to do before the dawn of Christmas arrives."

He certainly has a way with words and is unbelievably persuasive for his size. "Buddy, wait just one minute. I said the group obviously wants to do this. I am with you guys, but we must plan each step carefully. What do we need from the garage?" "Belts and ropes. Anything that will be useful for the harnesses. We need the blankets and things to keep Misty and Abby warm on the sleigh." Buddy answered. "How do we get to the garage without everyone seeing us?" I asked. Buddy went on to tell us that silence was the key. We go up the stairs and make a sharp left into the laundry room. Once in there, the dog door opens into the garage.

"Oh sure, your dog door is going to fit us." Ben broke in. "No, the door was here when I got to this house and I never use it. I can't get out it's too high. However, I have a little secret I keep from the folks. If I push the laundry detergent box over to the opening, I can get out into the garage when I like. The same goes for the door in the garage that goes outside. I have things I can push up to them. The folks would never let me out alone, but sometimes I enjoy a little stroll around the grounds."

"Buddy, old sport, you surprise me." Laughed Deacon. "I never would have suspected you could be so devious."

"Let's go!" I said, "Buddy lead the way." Up the stairs we went. If the folks didn't hear my heart thumping, they couldn't hear anything. Into the laundry room, into the garage without a hitch.

Chapter 9

The garage was unreal, neat and tidy. I couldn't believe it was a garage. When I thought of the condition of the one at home, I was amazed.

I must admit, ours is much more interesting and exciting. There are some very unusual and fascinating things in our garage. You can't find a darn thing unless you move everything and back out any vehicles that are parked there. Here, we didn't have to run around looking for things because all were in their proper places. Several coils of rope hung on the back wall. "Smokey, jump up on the work bench and grab that big loop of light brown rope and the white cord as well.

Take down those two rolls of duck tape on that peg by the shelf." "Oh Bud, where are the belts?" "Hanging in that closet." Ben got the door open and sure enough neatly hanging on small hooks were about fifteen belts of various styles and colors. "Grab about 10 or 12 of the good leather ones." Deacon yelled. "Make sure they're the longest." Buddy disappeared into the big closet and called out for Shannon and Dakota to follow him. "Here's a blanket for each of you to carry." He stood on his hind legs and reached as high as he could to the shelf holding the blankets. He grabbed the first one and pulled it down and then got the second one. "Okay girls, don't get these full of snow on the way down the hill." "Don't call us girls." Shannon snapped, "We have names." "Sorry, no offense meant." "None taken." Dakota said, "My mother is a feminist." Misty hurried to be the peacemaker again. "Now, now, this is not the time for such nonsense. We are all equal in this endeavor. That was made clear from the start. Shannon you know Buddy meant absolutely nothing by that term. If anything, it's more a term of endearment than anything else." "Okay, Okay. Maybe I did over react. I guess it's all the excitement." Shannon explained.

Buddy once again entered the closet with Smoky following close behind him. A few minutes later Smoky emerged with a small sheep skin rug. Buddy came out and pushed the door shut. "We need that sheep skin for the bottom of the sleigh, so don't drag it through the snow."

"Time out everyone." I said. I felt I had to try and keep reminding them this was no game. "Let's organize our gear and make sure we have everything we need." Buddy walked across the garage and pushed a small wooden box in front of the dog door. "Hey, Bear, see that canvas bag hanging on the nail by the end of the work bench?" "Yes." I answered. "Well grab it. We might need it." "What's in it?" "Snacks, they think I don't know where they keep them." He jumped up on the box and turned toward the rest of us. "Are we ready? Let's go!" "Hold your horses, little one. We have to make a final check. Get off that box and slide it back. You're going out at the end of the line."

Buddy was too excited to organize or check anything. He slid the box back. I took command. "Deacon, you lead and break trail for us." "Great, but where do I lead? I don't know for sure where we're heading." "Just go out this door, go to your left staying as close to the building as you can, when you get to the corner turn left again and go to the corner of the house. Wait there until we all catch up. When we're ready to cross the yard we'll all go at once, but, single file mind you. Misty, you and Buddy each carry a roll of tape. Buck, take some of those belts. Ben, you and Deacon each get a loop of rope. I'll take the bag and the rest of the belts. We'll go out as follows: Deacon, Buck, Ben, Shannon, Dakota, Smoky, Misty, Buddy and I'll bring up the rear. With everyone going ahead the trail will be pretty well packed down for Misty and Buddy.

"One last thing. I want each of you to bow your heads and silently ask your God or higher power to be with us in this venture. We need all the help we can get." It got so quiet I thought they had all quit breathing. I lifted my head when my prayer was finished and looked over the team. They had become a team. Maybe a RAG TAG team, but definitely a team. Gradually, all heads had lifted and the eyes that looked back at me were different. These dogs are going to do it. Without a second thought, I nudged Deacon and said, "Let's go!"

CHAPTER 10

As we stood at the corner of the house, near the little deck off the den, I caught a glimpse of the fire. It was still burning and little fingers of flames waved us on. I like to think it was wishing us "Good Luck".

I told the others to stay perfectly still while I moved over to some bushes for a better look at the upstairs. It was just as I thought. The tree was in the corner of the living room. It was great and beautiful, decorated in sparkling lights and an array of colorful garlands. I pictured myself stretched out in front of it, gazing absent mindedly at the lights, enjoying the season. Not tonight, old boy. If all goes well you can lay in front of your own tree tomorrow night.

I could see our people walking around, stopping here and there to visit with someone. They were laughing and talking totally unaware of what was happening right beneath them. Little Kirk toddled over to the window, looked down and saw me. I stood stock still, frozen in place. He waved. Then he began pounding on the window. Jake came up and took him by the hand and led him away. I went back to the others. "That was close, let's go."

"What do you think, Deacon? Straight across or hang to the tree line?" I asked. "Straight across. Ready? Here we go!" With that, he was off across the yard, snow flying up around his feet. Tight behind were Buck and the other bigger ones. By the time Buddy and Misty started, the path was fairly easy for them to maneuver. When I reached the bushes on the far side of the yard I looked back. I could still see the folks up at the house. I sincerely hoped we would all see each other in the morning.

The hill was quite steep and near the top the undergrowth was thick. About half way down Buddy lost his footing. He scrambled hard in an attempt to regain it, but he was sliding fast. I yelled, "Deacon, help him." Deacon looked up and with a flying leap threw himself sideways into the snow and the path of Buddy's sure destruction. As Deacon lay there, Buddy slammed into him with a thud. The force pushed Deacon ever so slightly. I was afraid they would start to slide, but they held. Buddy got up carefully, slowly he shook himself. "Nothing broke. No worse for the wear. Thanks, Deacon, I owe you one." "Our hero!" Shannon yelled, "Where are your blue tights and cape?" "Knock it off." Ben said, "Don't be a twit." "I didn't mean anything. I just wanted to make a little joke." Shannon explained. "Lighten up everybody. We've a long way to go." The going was slower from then on. Perhaps we were just being more cautious.

A few minutes passed and we were on level ground right in somebody's back yard. There were lights on in the house and we could hear the faint sound of Christmas music. I whispered softly "Buddy, where's the sleigh?" "It's down two more houses." "Are you sure it's there?" "Yes, I saw it earlier today."

As we crept along in the shadows, our ears, eyes and noses were alert to every sound, sight and smell. We were on a mission. This was serious business. Suddenly, Buddy's voice broke the silence. "There it is! There it is!"

Hard to make out in the dark, I went closer. Oh dear Lord. When I clapped my big black eyes on that sleigh, my heart sunk. We're sunk. It was a regular old-fashioned kids sleigh with steel runners, a steering bar and an old wooden box nailed to the back half. It was about six feet long, and in faded paint I could read the words "Flying Carpet" written across the steering bar. We're going to need a magic carpet, I though, but I kept silent.

The sleigh was tipped up against an old garage. I turned and looked toward the house next to it, but there were no lights on and no signs of activity. That's a good break, I thought, at least we can work here unobserved.

The sleigh had a rope attached on the ends of the steering bar. This was for pulling the sleigh under ordinary conditions. We picked up the rope and draped it over the front of the box. Using this rope, Buddy could direct the sleigh by pulling left or right. Hopefully, using this method, the sleigh would follow us. We, in turn (ideally speaking) would be following whoever was the lead. Actually, it was a difficult decision between Buck and Deacon. The final vote went to Buck. Only because, of all things, he was wearing a harness. Buck told me when traveling he wears a harness for rest area stops because Mike finds it easier to handle him.

We had already checked, the harness would also fit Deacon. Deacon agreed to be lead if Buck found it too hard or not to his liking.

We pulled the sleigh over to the tracks and got it situated

between the rails. Next, we took the rope we brought from the garage and folded it in half. The two ends were placed near the front of the sleigh. We then gently straightened the remainder of the rope. It was about 20 feet long folded. "Buck, take that harness off. Deacon, help him. Put the harness at the end of the rope. Here, Ben, take this end and carry it to the harness. Thread it through the ring on the back and bring it back here to the front of the sleigh." With that done we tied the two end pieces of rope to the metal part just in front of the steering bar. We made sure the knots wouldn't interfere with the steering.

About five feet from the front of the sleigh we belted and taped the lead rope together. Moving another five feet, we did the same thing and finally at the next five-foot mark, we belted and taped again. That gave us four distinct sections. We took our collars off to hook a belt and some cord to them. The belts were connected to the lead rope on the inside, while the long pieces of cord were tied on the outside of the collars to run under our bodies between the front and back legs. Then the cord and belt would be attached to the lead rope in the same location.

Chapter 11

I must be losing it, I thought. Every time I glanced back at the power plant, with all the lights and vapors raising into the night air, I would get a little uneasy about our adventure.

Somehow the big sprawling plant looked safe and secure. Just as the freighter unloading at the dock looked powerful and confident. Safe, secure, powerful and confident, all the things I didn't feel. I only gave myself the luxury of a couple of seconds to look and got right back to the business at hand.

We had almost finished. Buck, Buddy, and Misty worked feverishly to get us all re-collared and hooked. Buddy was helping Buck into his harness and Misty was checking the knots, buckles, and duct tape to make sure all was secure and in order. They both stepped back for a better look. The "team" stood very still. Buddy and Misty walked up one side of the team and down the other. "You all look marvelous!" she cried. "So very beautiful and handsome. I am so proud to be part of this effort. I never dreamed at my age I would ever be involved with such an adventure." With that she dabbed at one eye and then the other. "I am so happy."

Buddy, never at a loss for words, kept prancing, and I mean prancing, back and forth. Finally he said, "I can't believe it's really happening. You guys look positively professional. You look great. We're going to be famous. We are, I know we are." He paused to catch his breath. "Dear cousins, thank you for making this my greatest hour. Words cannot express how I feel at this moment. We are entering into history."

"Buddy, please! Just knock it off and let's get started before I really get cold feet." That Shannon, she has a way with words.

"God speed." Buddy yelled as he jumped into the box and picked up the rope to the steering bar.

Heavens above. Are we actually going to try and move this sleigh? Are we really going to head off into God knows what? Just in case the Lord was busy listening to other prayers when I said mine in the garage, I sent another prayer up to be on the safe side.

Buddy leaned over the front of the box and whispered, "Bear, should I count to three and have you guys start on that?" "Ya, that'll be fine, little friend." I looked at Ben, but couldn't read his thoughts. He nodded, telling me he heard and understood. I called to each team. "Smoke, Shannon, on the count of three, Deacon, Dakota, on the count of three, Buck, on the count of three". They answered individually in the affirmative. I took a deep breath, looked heavenward, closed my eyes, opened them. I was ready.

We had discussed earlier how we would start walking and keep that up until we felt we could move up to a slow trot. All agreed there would be no running until everyone felt comfortable. Where in the heck did we get these ideas? It was frightening to think about it.

"Bear, do you realize we have neither stars nor moon to help guide up." The remark startled me. "Ben, even if the moon and stars were visible, I doubt any of us could use them for direction." "Well, even if we couldn't tell direction by them, a night sky full of stars and the smallest sliver of the moon would be comforting." "Your right on that point, Ben." He looked worried. He shook his big head and said, "Good luck, partner. I am ready when you are." "Good luck yourself, partner." I said, and with that I turned and nodded at Buddy.

Buddy's voice barked out "one", it sounded strong, confident and commanding, "two", you'd never realize his size by the sound of his voice alone, "three". The sleigh jerked forward as we took the first steps. We were actually moving along. I've heard Arne use a term quite often that covers our first movements. "Steady by jerks, steady by jerks." I said it a couple of times in my head and figured there were several ways to interpret that. I looked up and could see Buck with his tail curled proudly up over his back. He looked stately and all business, he was walking exactly in the middle of the tracks. Deacon and Dakota were in pretty close step. No trouble there. Smoky was having some trouble, he kept looking at Shannon's feet and trying to match her step. "Smoky, Smoky – No! Don't turn around, just listen. Find your own walking style and soon you and Shannon will be doing fine. Don't watch her. Try and sense her movements, but don't look at her. See, you're doing much better. Keep your eyes on the trail ahead."

We were actually going forward. Houses and trees were coming and going and we were moving. We were moving. We were moving. The words sing songed through my head.

"Good grief!" Shannon yelled, "What are we on?" "Take care, calm yourself. It's a train bridge." "A train bridge? What's that?" she asked. "Exactly what I said. It's a bridge that crosses water or roads and is strong enough to carry a train." If that wasn't the most simplistic explanation I'd ever given about something. Again Shannon let loose, "Yikes! Look at the water." "Don't look down! Keep your head up!" Ben yelled, "And be quiet." Dakota started making strange little noises and mumbling about water.

Finally, when no one picked up on her quiet little comments, she yelled, "I hate water and I am not crossing another of these darn things. "The Plan" said nothing about water." I called to Deacon to keep talking to her and explain we were perfectly safe. Safe. Somehow, using that word at a time like this seemed ridiculous.

I really expected Smoky to be all trembly and scared, but he was doing just fine. I watched him. He appeared to be all business. Everyone was concentrating very hard on the job at hand. It wasn't easy. It was something I would compare to learning to dance on ice blind folded. Dealing with a partner plus the other team members. Ya! That's it I thought, a dance troupe. You and your partner must work like one and blend in with the others to perform in perfect harmony.

We hadn't blended quite yet. Jerks and tugs. Stumbles and bumbles. Looking up and briefly scanning those ahead, I knew none of us had ever worked harder. At this point, no one was uttering a sound.

Meet The "Team"

Bear
Arne & Julie Hayes-Moe
Munising, Michigan

Abby
"Old Mama" Gert Hayes
Rapid River, Michigan

Buck
Dr. Mike & Kathy Hayes
Lauren & Jacob
Waukee, Iowa

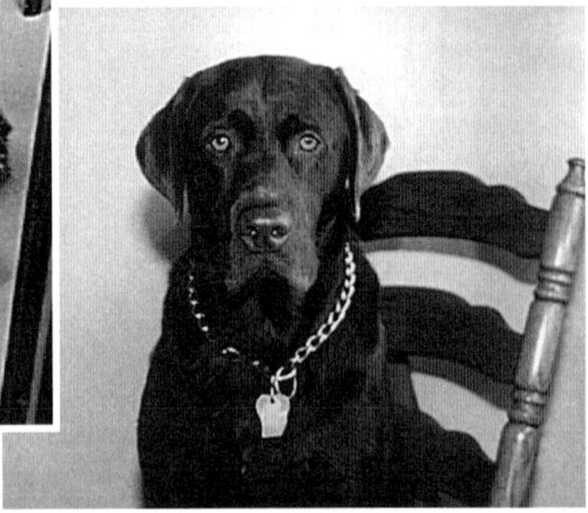

Deacon
Peter & Merrylie Hayes
Jason, Mike, Josh & Larry
Tustin, Michigan

Buddy
Bill & Anita Hayes
Greg & Mary Hayes
Marquette, Michigan

Misty
Dr. Bill & Maggie Kline
Scott, David & Kim,
Lynn Marie
Green Bay, Wisconsin

Ben
Jim & Phyllis Steele
Mary Hayes-Carlson
Sault Ste. Marie, Michigan

Shannon & Dakota
Kirk & Mary Hayes Nigro
Mary & Joe Guckenberg
Sean Allen & Kirkie
Ishpeming, Michigan

Jacob & Tabers
Waukee, Iowa

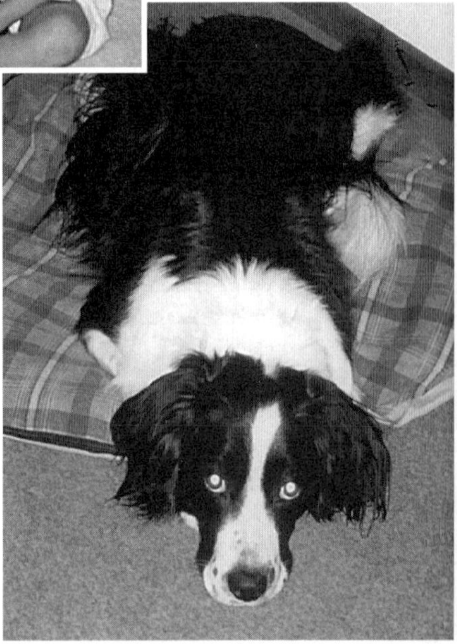

Smoky
Arne & Julie Hayes-Moe
Munising, Michigan

Chapter 12

I suppose in an effort to keep everyone at ease and keep our minds off what we were doing, Buddy started a running commentary on the places we were passing.

"We have just crossed Carp River where it flows into the greatest and largest inland lake in the United States, Lake Superior, which is located on our left. To the right is the sewage disposal plant." Believe it or not, not one nasty comment was made. In fact, no one said a word. The team was really getting into this. The going was slow, but we were really trying for a rhythm.

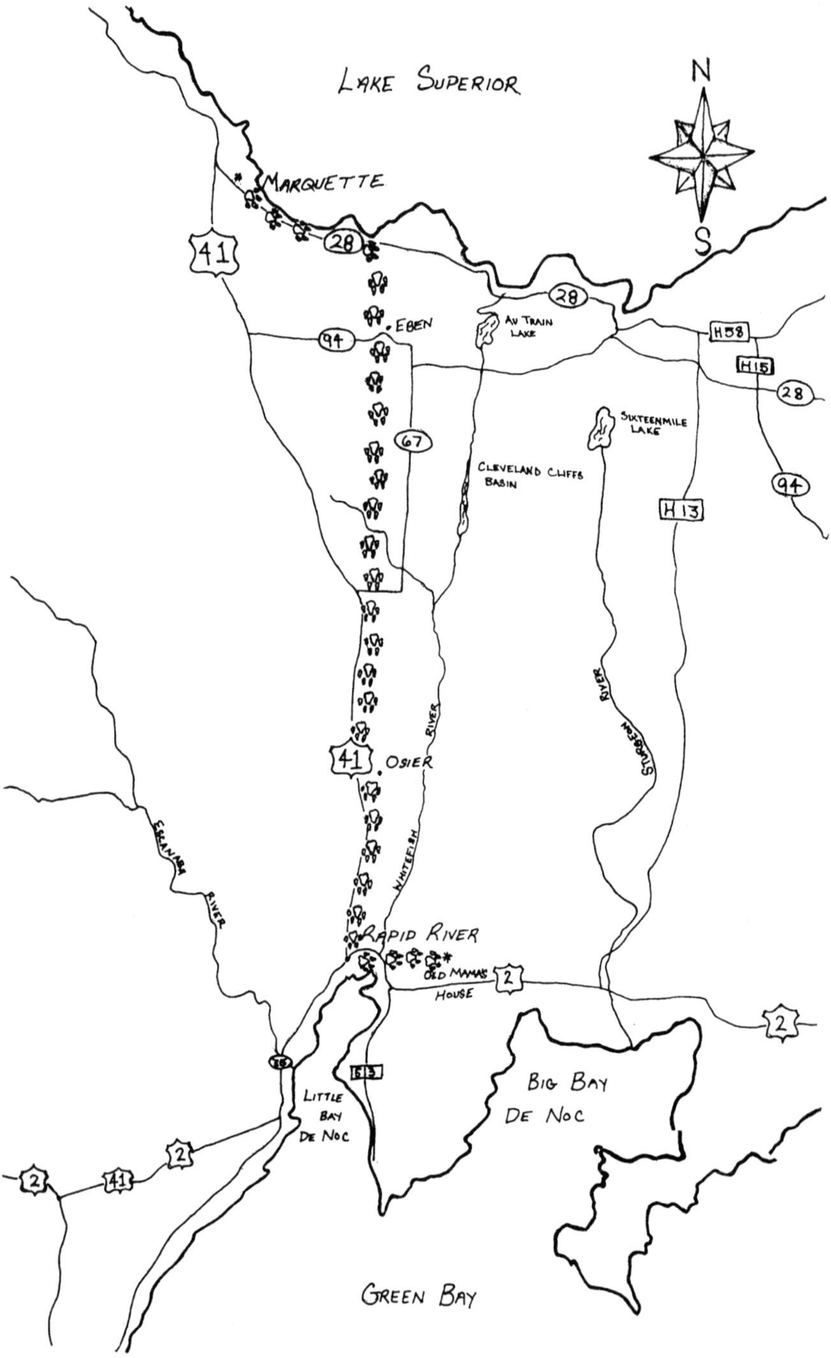

LAKE SUPERIOR
N
S
MARQUETTE
41
28
EBEN
94
AU TRAIN LAKE
H58
H15
67
SIXTEENMILE LAKE
CLEVELAND CLIFFS BASIN
94
H13
RIVER
STURGEON
41
OSIER
RIVER
WHITEFISH
ESCANABA
RIVER
RAPID RIVER
OLD MAMA'S HOUSE
2
2
LITTLE BAY DE NOC
BIG BAY DE NOC
2
41
2
GREEN BAY

Buddy continued, "We are now in front of the gates to Marquette State Prison. Ike Wood, an uncle of our folks, wrote a book about this place after working there for many years. It's called "One Hundred Years at Hard Labor".

I wondered how much information was tucked into that little brown head. How long would it take for us to be overloaded with his travel log? It didn't take much longer. When we passed the big log building that is an information and rest stop, Shannon said, "Buddy, I don't know how to say this without insulting you, but if you don't bag it, and bag it now, I might do something foolish. Like tossing you off the next train bridge which, I believe, is coming up now." With that Dakota stopped. We all stopped. "I am not crossing that dang thing." "Listen to me, young lady." Shannon growled, "We signed on with this team and we are going to see it through. You are not quitting before we actually get started. Now move it girl, or I'll give you a nip in the butt." "But, Ma!" whined Dakota, "I am afraid of water." "Well it's not water anymore. It's ice. So move it!"

Deacon reached over and licked Dakota's ear and began talking softly to her. Without further adieu, Deacon yelled, "Let's go!" We slowly moved on.

It was amazing. We were actually making headway. We had passed over several small bridges. They were hardly recognized as such with the water underneath frozen and all the snow and bushes around. I had caught a glimpse of a really big one coming up, bigger than any thus far. Be prepared, I said to myself. So I took the "bull by the horns" so to speak. "Deacon, bridge up ahead. Talk to that partner of yours." "Will do." "Shannon, help Dakota anyway you can." "I will, but take a look at that thing. It's really long. Hey, this is a big river and there's no ice." "Shannon, don't work yourself up. Keep calm." I couldn't believe my ears when I heard Smoky telling Shannon to keep her head up and not be afraid. "This bridge has sides on it. We can't fall off." Crossing the bridge we scarcely took a breath. It was big and the black waters under it were moving rapidly along. I think we moved as one, we were concentrating so hard on getting over in one piece.

Thank God! The bridge was behind us. Houses with back yards facing the railroad were lining much of the track now. Wonderfully pungent aromas drifted from the houses. Holiday meals were my favorite because a table treat was much more likely. Although, I must admit, picnics and cookouts were a close second. Most of the yards were fenced and several dogs stood looking at us like we were from another planet. In one yard a big Dalmatian yelled to his neighbors, "Hey, come here. Take a look at this." A little Beagle mix crawled out of his house and ran to the fence. "What are you guys up to? Where you going? Hey, wait!" Turning to his neighbor, the Dalmatian, I heard him say, "Lots of those teams are snooty." He called us a team. I heard him, he actually said "team".

CHAPTER 13

The houses gave way to the woods. Occasionally we were able to see distant lights and I assumed them to be houses.

I again caught the faint odor of food cooking. Hope they enjoy their meal. I wonder if we'll ever see another?

On we trekked. The woods were dark, but the clouds appeared to be breaking up. It is amazing how much light the snow provides and how it improves visibility.

WHOOSH—Buck jumped. We all stopped! "What the heck was that? Did you guys see it? It was huge!" Buck turned toward us and you could tell he was rattled.

Deacon started to howl with laughter and laid down. I thought whatever it was had also startled him, but I was wrong. Deacon just thought it was hilarious that Buck, who hadn't made a false move since we started and had taken the lead position so seriously, was rattled. "Darn it, Deacon," I yelled, "what was that?" "It's probably one of the biggest snowy owls I've ever seen." He said. "It's sitting on the lower branch of that big pine directly behind us on the left." We all turned to look and sure enough, there it sat. A huge creature, sort of an off white color with big eyes and an ugly beak. It fixed us with an unblinking stare. Very unnerving. The large head turned slowly once or twice, but I got the impression the eyes still watched us. Again, it looked squarely at us. This time it spoke. "What are you doing out here at this time of night without a human? What kind of a team are you?"

There was that word again. Owls are supposed to be wise and he called us a team. Buck had regained his composure and said, "We're on a mission to get a friend." "Nicely put, Buck, I couldn't have said it better myself." The owl turned his head several times and again looked back to us. "Well, good luck on your trip, but please hurry through my territory. I am out here looking for a holiday meal." Did that bird laugh? I couldn't tell.

I looked to Smoky. He didn't really appear to pay much attention to the owl. He was definitely having some problems. His ears kept going flat to his head, a sure sign of trouble for him. "Are you okay, Smoky?" I asked. He looked quickly toward the woods again and said, "I guess so." Ben said, "He's been watching the woods for quite awhile, ever since we passed all the houses." Buddy called out, "Let's get this show on the road. We've a long way to go yet."

Again we started. The evening was becoming more pleasant, the night sky was clearing quickly. There is nothing so breathtaking or awe inspiring as a black sky with millions and millions of stars reflecting their sparkling faceted light. The only way to view the sky like this is when there is no man made light to interfere. Looking up into a sky like this truly makes one feel insignificant.

CHAPTER 14

We were moving again and all appeared to be okay. Smoky tripped slightly, but caught himself. Something was up with him, but I couldn't figure out what.

Oh wow, what a magnificent sight. Standing on a small knoll to the right of us stood two wolves watching our approach with unabashed interest. As we pulled abreast of them, I heard one ask, "What are they?" "Dogs", came the one word answer. "Dogs?" "Yes, dogs. They were like us centuries ago, but their ancestors took to man. They became his friend, companion, helper, and hunter. Whatever. Basically they're like us." "They don't look like us. They're all different. Nothing about them matches, not size, shape or color. They can't be like us. They can't be wolves." "I said they started out as wolves." The larger of the two took a couple of steps toward us. He raised his head and let out a long haunting howl. We stood mesmerized by the sound. He paused and again let loose with that haunting, gut tingling sound. I noticed a couple of the team were shifting and moving like their harnesses and collars were becoming uncomfortable. "Easy guys", I thought, "don't let this Knight of the Forest get to you". I had the feeling there were a couple more standing in the darkness behind these two, but I couldn't make them out. "You're wolves. I can't believe it." said Deacon. "Of all the time I've spent in the woods you're the first I've ever seen." The wolves stared back, but didn't answer. Buck summoned the courage to talk to them. "Good for you Buck" I thought, "don't let them intimidate you". "What are you guys doing out here tonight?" he demanded. No answer. The air was heavy with centuries of separation. I got the impression the wolves didn't want to speak with us. I thought, "Well, I'll be darned, they think they're superior to us". Shannon finally found her voice, "Hey! Where's your manners? The least you could do is answer us? Who do you think you are? I know about wolves. You're only good for running down poor little deer and other animals to eat." "Shannon!" the tone of Ben's voice told me he was really upset with her. "Stop that line of talk or you and I are going to have a serious face to face." "Well, they're being ignorant." Deacon turned toward Shannon, "You, lady, need a lesson in living in the wild. Keep in mind they don't get a bowl of Kibbles and a pail of water set in front of them each night."

The wolves didn't appear in the least upset with Shannon's remarks. I thought they were about to leave, but the big one raised his head and gave another heart thumping howl. He lowered his head. He fixed me with a strange look that said explain to your pack who we are and what we're about. At that moment I felt a stirring in my spirit for him and his kind. I knew how they were hated and feared, hunted down for no reason other than because they were wolves. Over the centuries man became so fearful and paranoid about wolves that the line between fact and fiction fused. Man figured he had no use for wolves. Could it be because wolves had no use for man? I felt things could get a little out of hand and rather quickly. Poor understanding of a situation can often result in a confrontation. That's the last thing I wanted to happen. "Listen up folks, you heard what they said about us. That at one time we were like them. We choose a life apart from the pack, away from nature and the elements. That doesn't make us right or wrong. Nor does it make them right or wrong. Basically, he's correct, we are very similar. Think back, you've all heard stories where one or more of us have reverted. Think kindly on our wild brothers and sisters and wish them a long and healthy life."

When I finished my little speech I turned, fully expecting a nod of approval from our nighttime visitors. To my dismay they had receded back into the woods and darkness.

"Weren't they spectacular! I never thought we'd bump into a couple of wolves." Deacon was really excited about seeing them. Most of the others were simply in awe of the encounter and nothing much was said. Finally, Buddy broke the spell and ordered us forward.

CHAPTER 15

The woods and bushes were passing so quickly, I couldn't believe we were traveling so fast. Every once in awhile I thought I heard tiny bells but I didn't want to break my concentration to search out the source.

The dark jack pine stands and willow bushes along the track were giving way to stands of hardwoods. Buddy hollered, "Bear, we'll be leaving the railroad grade in a few minutes."

As it had done several times already, the sleigh came to a clumsy but very abrupt halt. "Smoky, what's the matter with you? Why do you keep stopping? What on earth are you looking at? You've been doing just great. You and Shannon have moved right along and appear to be working well together. Now tell me, kid, what's eating you? What's the problem?" Smoky had his head down and looked ashamed. "I'm sorry. I really haven't meant to hold us up, but they're following us!" "Who's following us?" I asked, looking wildly around thinking a couple of strays may have fallen in behind us. The wolves! I hate to admit, but the thought did cross my mind.

Everyone by this time was looking in every direction and could see nothing. Buck called from the front, "There's nothing up here and I haven't noticed anything." "Nothing out of the ordinary for Dakota and me. We haven't noticed anyone or anything. Do you want me to look around a bit more?" "Smoky's been shaking and trembling for the last few miles," Shannon said, "but he wouldn't let me tell. He said he was okay."

The area where we had stopped was still a blend of medium sized evergreens and hardwoods. The railroad bed was built up and there was a fairly good size ditch on either side of the track. The sky had cleared and the few remaining clouds hung very low on the eastern horizon. Things were quite visible for the night. It was unearthly quiet. I'm not used to the silence of the woods in winter. It wasn't frightening, but it did speed ones imagination. The woods can appear to hold all kinds of interesting forms. As I looked again, where Smoky indicated someone was following, I thought for a moment I saw something. Buddy said, "Okay, we've wasted enough time. Let's get with the program. We have a long way to go. We're not quite to our turn off for Eben."

Holy wha! My mind had been on several hundred diverse subjects since we started this trip, and I never for a moment felt we would make a mile let alone get past Sand River. How on earth did we get this far? I couldn't believe it. "Buddy, are you sure where we are?" "Yes, we passed our camp and Sand River. I know where we are. It's like a miracle we're making such fantastic time." It had to be a miracle. We couldn't possibly have done it by ourselves. Buddy called out, "Is everyone ready? Count of three again? Let's get truckin'. We're doing great!"

Chapter 16

I was allowing myself the pleasurable thought of the possibility of the success of this endeavor. The thrill of the run was beginning to fill the very fiber of my being.

The team, our team, was racing along without a hitch. The hesitation and jerkiness of the start was gone. There was a great feeling of exhilaration and fluidity of motion. This in turn had created a sense of well being, of power, of control. I was totally into this dog team business. I looked ahead at the group. Was this a dream or was it really happening?

Again I thought I could hear the faint tinkling of bells but I was feeling so fast and free, I paid no attention. My harness felt like it was made especially for me. It no longer pulled and tugged at my coat like when we first started.

We'd only covered a short distance, when from the front Buck yelled, "Halt!" We stopped so fast we bumped into one another and the sleigh slid into Ben and I. "What the heck's going on?" Ben asked. "Darned if I know, but we'll find out quick enough." "Buck, why'd you stop us?" I didn't get a reply, so I called to Deacon. "What's going on, Deacon? Is Buck okay?" "Yes, everything's fine. Come up here." I slipped out of my harness and walked forward. Standing right smack in front of Buck was a huge deer. He was dark gray and looked ancient. His head was lowered at Buck and they were almost nose to nose. He only had one antler. It was a fine specimen of half a rack. With both he must have been a regal sight. Buck was doing alright. His legs were stiff and his body taut, but his tail was down slightly indicating he wasn't ready to take this challenge on just yet. The deer was really big and when I got a good look at him I wanted to laugh, but knew it wouldn't be polite nor politically correct. Standing next to Deacon, I asked him, "You're the woods and water guy on this team, what's going on?" Deacon said, "As far as I can figure he comes with his ladies to drink from that small spring that feeds into the ditch. Buck and the rest of us are standing in his territory. He wants us out!" "Oh. So what are we supposed to do? And is Buck or anyone of us in any immediate danger?" "No danger if we get our backsides out of here on his terms." "What are his terms?" "Leave quickly and quietly. Now!" Deacon went on, "I'll handle it. Hey, Sport, we didn't realize we were intruding on anyone's space. If you step aside, we'll be happy to get out of here. By the way, that's one part of a handsome rack you carry. I'll bet you can tell stories that could curl hair about narrow escapes and close encounters of the ugly type." The big buck raised his head and looked at Deacon. "I'll bet I couldn't stare you down like I did the young one here?" "Well, I don't know." Deacon replied, "You're pretty tough looking and I don't think you've lost very many skirmishes." The buck tossed his head and gave a snort. "You know, brown dog, you're pretty clever. You got my mind off your friend and made me realize I had no reason for fear or anger. Where are you dogs going? How come you don't have any hunters with you?" "Why would we have hunters with us?" It was Dakota that asked such an innocent question. "Dogs are always with hunters." The buck answered matter of factly. Deacon leaned over to Dakota and whispered to her. She looked up at the buck and nodded her head. "We're on our way to get a friend and were losing time." It was Buddy, all business and not the least bit intimidated by the buck. "Sorry we bothered you, but we simply must be on our way." The buck stepped out from between the tracks and effortlessly leaped the ditch. "Have a good trip, dogs. You're welcome anytime, without hunters of course."

Before I headed back to my harness I asked Deacon what he told Dakota. He said, "I told her when the deer said hunters, he meant humans."

Back in the harness, Buddy gave the start count. We were off! I couldn't help thinking this was a night to remember. Little did I know that something even more memorable was about to transpire.

CHAPTER 17

I could hear Buddy calling me. "I can hear you little friend. Go ahead, what is it?" "We'll be leaving the tracks shortly. The turn off will be a well traveled snowmobile trail off to the right of us. I'll have us slow before the turn."

The words were barely out of his mouth when I saw Smoky looking to the left with a wild look in his eye. He stumbled and the sled and team came to a very ungraceful stop. I was getting very upset with Smoky and I know the others were too. I was just about to give him a good scolding when he said, "Bear, look! Across the ditch."

I turned, as did the rest. At first I couldn't make out anything. Then, slowly they came into view. There standing on the far side of the ditch in the shadows of the trees were at least ten, maybe as high as 15 dogs of various breeds, mixed breeds, sizes, shapes and colors. Where in the heck did they come from? Why didn't we see them? Why didn't we smell them, or hear them? Every one of us stiffened, bristled slightly and prepared for a confrontation. Even though nobody moved, we were ready. For what, I didn't know.

Who are they? Where'd they come from? What are they doing here? We were all whispering questions. "They're ghosts!" "What?" "They're ghosts!" Misty said. She had gotten off the sleigh and was standing next to me. "How do you know?" I asked. "Simple! I've lived in Indian territory long enough to know a ghost when I see one. They can't talk to us I'll bet. They're harmless!" "Thank you, Misty for sharing that bit of trivia with us." Shannon said. "But I'm keeping my guard up."

"Look! Oh my gosh, look!" Dakota, the one who always looked worried, was bright eyed and smiling. "Look at the sleigh. Look at our harnesses. They're beautiful!"

The dogs standing in the shadows across the ditch were momentarily forgotten. As we all examined and admired our new sleigh and harnesses. The sleigh was positively the most beautiful thing I'd ever seen. A work of art. It was very similar to the dog sleds that are made at Superior Sleds in Chatham by Dave and Ellen Robison.

A sled made by them but all fancied up with rawhide back and sides by Iverson's in Shingleton. Iverson's make snowshoes, lodge furniture and other wonderful things of bent wood and rawhide. The harnesses were made of sturdy soft leather and the connecting points were secured with copper rivets. There was a small, silver bell attached by a ribbon to the outside of each of our individual harnesses. There was no sign of the old sleigh. The ropes, belts and duct tape were gone. It was breathtaking! It was a miracle! Now I knew why we were doing so well and the distance flew by. Heaven rode with us.

Suddenly my thoughts snapped back to the dogs across the ditch. A hundred new scenarios went through my head, none good. Who were they and what did they want? I was relieved to see that they hadn't taken the opportunity to pull a sneak attack while we were distracted by our new gear. No, there they stood silently watching us. As we stood gawking, a medium size brown and black hound type moved toward us. The dog walked over to a dead tree laying partly across the ditch. "They could cross there if they wanted" I thought. One good jump would put them right next to us. The others remained where they were. The hound moved out further on the tree; stopped, and looked at each of us. Not as a group, but as individuals. The dog appeared to be studying us. Perhaps looking for our weaknesses. No, these dogs weren't a threat. I could feel that. What was going on? Was Misty right? Were they ghosts? The way they blended into the background, they sure looked like ghosts.

The dog standing on the dead tree began to speak. Oh boy! So much for non-talking ghosts. "My name is Queen. I belonged to your folks when they were just children." What! I'd never heard of Queen. She must come from a really long time ago. "I was a stray. Hungry and tired, I wandered into the little town where they lived. Billy took me home. I still remember the words. Probably the most beautiful words I'd ever heard. "Mama, can I keep her, Mama, can I keep her?" The answer was "yes"! I had a home. I was loved. Oh, for so many years I had Billy and a family." "Billy? That's my human dad's name." Buddy squealed. "Yes, I know." Said Queen. " Max told me." "Max! I've heard of him. Is he with you? Let me see him. I want to talk with him. I have so many things to tell him." "No, you can't talk with him, but you can see him. Look, there he is." Sure enough, up by the edge of the woods stood a little black and tan dachshund. He jumped up on his hind legs a couple of times then dropped and ran back and forth. The picture of health and exuberance. "He's very happy to see you." Said Queen, "And he sends greetings to the folks."

As my eyes became accustomed to the darkness, by the edge of the trees I could begin to make out distinct sizes, shapes and colors. So they were ghosts. Oh brother, now what? I couldn't help it. I started looking for those I would know. The big red and white Bassett. That had to be Jennie. I couldn't help staring at her, I never saw such gigantic ears on a dog. Those two big German Shepherds had to be Schooner and Ceasar. Standing off together were two magnificent Labradors. Their pale gold color told me one was Tabers and the other Levi. The big Irish Setter running and playing with a Malamute must be Shannon. The Malamute had to be Kiko, the fish sandwich dog. I was stumped as to some of the others. The biggest dog I've ever seen was the all white one. He looked like he could be Malamute. I couldn't be positive, but he was big. He stood apart from the rest, like he was special or maybe just aloof. There was a smaller version of a German Shepherd type with a curled up tail and bright piercing eyes. I guess it was more his coloring that made me think of a Shepherd. No special breed, just dog. He was sitting, watching us with great interest. The last dog I could make out was a medium size tan and white. The dog had short legs, was stocky, sort of a Border Collie type with a nice tail and Spaniel shaped face. That's most likely where the coloring came from.

Queen spoke again. "We want you to know how happy we are about what you're doing. It tells us that the children I knew and the adults they became have made us proud. I guess we raised them right. Only one of us can speak to you and I, being the oldest. was picked. A couple have sent messages to some of their folks. Please listen carefully." Queen looked back at the silent ones as if intently listening and then turned to us. "The first message is for Jacob. Tabers says he loves you very much and he's so happy you have Buck to play with now. He says what happened was an accident and hopes when you get older you will understand. Levi says he is proud of his boys and hopes they continue to do well. He likes to think his running and playing with

them helped with their many athletic successes. Dingo says hello to Mama and Mike. I believe he's referring to the lady you call "Old Mama". Dingo had to be the dog that sat and watched us so intently. Yes, I was right. When Queen mentioned his name, he stood up. "Mister sends greetings to all and is especially happy that Peter, Mike and Bobbi have children of their own. He loved them so." Mister, that was a name I was familiar with, he worked the mink ranch. I scanned the dogs I didn't know. When my eyes stopped on the tan and white Collie type it laid down and slapped it's tail in a form of a greeting. "So you're Mister, old boy. Happy to make your acquaintance. I hear about you even though you're a real old timer."
Mister saved Julie and Peter from the attack of the "killer pig". Well, it wasn't really a killer, but it could've been, and if it had gotten to them it probably would have inflicted great harm. I'll be brief, but the story's worth telling.

Next to the mink ranch was a fairly good size pig farm. One of the brood sows got free and her litter followed. Unknown to Julie and little Pete, the pig was laying in the woods between the ranch and the farm with her little ones. The businesses were both fenced, but fortunately had utility gates in the back areas.

Julie, Pete and Mister were walking over to the pig farm to see the little ones. All of a sudden there was a horrible thrashing of the underbrush and the most awful squealing and snorting noise one could imagine. Julie looked up to see them being charged by the Mama pig.

Like a small sized pink freight train it came thundering out of the woods. Mister sprang into action. He attacked the pig. Julie grabbed Peter, ran to the fence and dropped him over. Then she ran to the gate. She kept hollering for Mister and finally he broke free and rushed through the gate to safety. His lip was cut, both ears were shredded and he had wounds on both front legs and shoulders. The vet couldn't believe what had happened to Mister. What a hero!

Queen gave several more messages and greetings and her last one identified the big white dog. "King, the dog by the stump, sends his best to Bill and thanks him for being a good friend. He wishes they could have had more time together. Time is getting short." She continued, "and we have much to do. Smoky has been able to see us since we began following you. We didn't mean to frighten you, Smoky. We know what you've been through. Time is a great healer and you will be fine".

"You have begun a wonderful adventure" Queen continued, "and you've done it for love and friendship; the right reasons. You call yourselves a Rag Tag team. Well, we are your shadow Rag Tag team, and if you don't mind, we'll run with you and share in your joy. All the years spent with each generation of children have made us what we are. That same passing of time has formed them into what they are and what they're about. All the laughter and tears, joy and sorrow, the sum total of our lives together, creating times like this. All of us and heaven too, run with you tonight. To the sleighs and the harnesses! We're off."

I watched in amazement as a sleigh exactly like ours, only larger, appeared out of nowhere. The shadow team stood in harness, ready to go. In their sleigh I could see Max, Jennie, and Peppi. Queen took up the reins of the sleigh. The lead dog was King. The matched partners were the Shepherds, Schooner and Ceasar, and the Labs, Tabers, and Levi. The mixed partners were Kiko and Shannon, Dingo and Mister. Together they made a beautiful team. The Rag Tag team and their shadow team were off.

We fairly flew over the trail, the tinkling of the small silver bells was the only sound. We had left the security of the railroad tracks. We didn't realize, but we probably didn't need them to keep us on the trail anyway. Our team held to the old woods road that was currently covered with snow and being used by the snowmobilers. The shadow team ran through the woods as if it were mist. It was an eerie yet comforting and wonderful sight. We all realized they were ghosts, but we weren't frightened. I figure ghosts are what you want them to be. If you want them friendly, so be it. If you want them scary, you can work that up too. As we flew through the woods, I thought about the shadow team. I got the impression they wanted this run as much as we did. A chance to return for a few minutes to their youth, to their memories of a time and place that was for them no more.

Thinking back to the messages that Queen had given, I wondered how we could possibly pass those along to our folks. I pondered that problem and after much deliberation I came to the conclusion that the messages couldn't be given verbally. The only way we could pass on the messages was by living good lives and sharing love with our folks. Queen and the Shadow Team must have realized this as well.

It occurred to me that suddenly the forest was alive with creatures watching us. It was as if someone had gone ahead announcing the great race to Rapid River.

Even with the Shadow Team and all the excitement of new harnesses and a new sleigh, Buddy was still in charge. He had regained the composure he displayed when we left the garage. "Bear, we will reach the Eben Junction in a matter of minutes. Then it's almost a straight shot to Rapid River."

CHAPTER 18

Seconds later we turned onto the old railroad grade. Long abandoned, with bushes and small trees crowding their way right up to the track bed, you couldn't mistake it for what it was.

The track out of Marquette had originally been Soo Line, but Wisconsin Central had purchased it and used it for several years before closing it. The track from Eben to Rapid River had also belonged to the Soo Line, but had been abandoned many, many years ago. The bridges over the small creeks and rivers had been torn up along with the tracks. That was no problem. We were flying! Not a paw or sleigh runner was touching the ground.

Out of Eben we went, past the big school into the open fields. I kept watching for something I might recognize. Finally, there it was, the huge barn on the old Vartti farm. Right in front of this farm, across the road, was Amanda Pitkamaki's old farm, the one my Arne spent so many happy days on working and playing as a boy. Arne's cousin, Ray, has the farm now. The barns on the Vartti and Pitkamaki farms are really quite unusual in the way they're built. The bottom section was made using cement and cedar blocks about a foot long. They look like a pile of wood with the spaces filled in with cement. When a door or a window casing was wanted the cedar blocks were split and the opening for the frame was made. This "wood pile" lower section held the milk stalls, grain rooms, calf pens and small equipment. The upper level was made in the ordinary fashion of the barns of that day. They had hip roofs providing a large hay storage area. These barns of cedar blocks and cement are warm and durable. Many are standing yet today. The Pitkamaki barn is over 65 years old.

In the time it took for me to relate that bit of information, we were at Trenary. I barely had a glimpse of the old potato warehouse with its colorful sign as we flew by. The smell of sweet cinnamon toast that the Trenary Bakery makes had to be a hunger pang. As we darted along, I spotted a couple of rabbits and even a fox snug and secure curled under branches and brush well away from the railroad bed. We fairly flew by a herd of beef cattle. They followed us with their big brown inquisitive eyes as only cattle can do.

As I looked over at Ben and on up to Smoky and Dakota, I swear they had such a look of pleasure on their faces, it was unreal. I glanced at the Shadow Team and saw the same look...no doubt about it

Pulling away from Trenary, I thought of the wonderful old black steam locomotives that charged up and down this very track for so many years. Bringing supplies, equipment and mail to people along its way. Returning with logs, lumber and heaven knows what all to the bigger cities. The stories those engines could tell.

On we sped. I can't say through the night—that's too limiting—more like through time.

Queen called to me, "Bear, when we stop, please have your team stop as well." "Okay!" I yelled, "Will do!" "Buddy, did you hear Queen?" "Yes , I did. But, why didn't she direct the message to me?" "Oh, I don't know for sure, but I wouldn't be concerned about it. Keep an eye on them to see when they stop." Buddy, a true professional, handled it well.

We passed through an area known as Osier, a long ago small settlement of woods workers and their families. Another family tie was here, our folks' maternal grandmother, Julia Grandchamp, was a school teacher in this little settlement in 1910. The schoolhouse still stands. It was there that she met her husband to be, Ernest LaViolette.

We crossed the Rapid River near the site of the Dutch Mill Park, a place of fond memories for our folks.

Many a family picnic was held there. Shortly I saw Queen give the high sign and both teams eased to a halt.

I looked around and immediately recognized where I was. We had stopped about a mile and a half from Old Mama's. To the left was the Grandchamp farm, as it stands today, and of course to the right would have been the area of the LaPine home. Old Mama was born on the Grandchamp farm. Her grandfather was a Grandchamp and her grandmother a La Pine.

Queen came over to us, "Please be patient with some of us. We have many strong and happy memories around here. Starting in this area all the way into Rapid River. My Billy and I often traveled this track. We fished at a little creek that crosses up the way. The farm holds good memories for Mister, as well as, myself. Mister was born there. Did you know that the children's great great grandfather homesteaded that farm in 1874?" "Yes, I know. Do you know that it's still owned by a cousin of our folks?" "Oh, that's wonderful. Do they still have cows and horses?" "No. I don't ever remember those."

The teams were moving again much slower, but still without any true effort on our parts. "There's the little creek I was telling you about. It runs into the Tacoosh River right over there." She nodded toward the west.

Chapter 19

We crossed the highway and in seconds we turned off the railroad bed practically into Old Mama's yard.

I looked at the house. Never in my wildest imagination did I believe we would actually stand in this spot on this night or any other night as far as that goes. We pulled the sleighs into the side yard. Most of the Shadow Team stepped from their harnesses and laid down. Silent and, for lack of a better term, respectful. Only Queen, Mister, Dingo and King stood watching the house.

The vertical blinds on the two big windows were flapping wildly around. From the outside it appeared that a small tornado was destroying the inside of the house. The barking was unbelievable. I had to remind myself it was only Abby. She didn't have a bunch of wild dogs helping her protect the house. I know what she does and what she sounds like from the inside, but I never actually heard and watched her act from the outside. It was really remarkable that one small dog could, excuse me, raise such *hell*.

The porch lights had been left on for the families late return. The colorful strings of Christmas lights around the roof of the porch were twinkling gaily and the big green wreaths with their huge red ribbons looked inviting. Shannon, Dakota, Ben and Deacon had started up to the porch. The curtains looked like they were being whipped by a huge beater. The volume on the barking went up several decibels.

"Hey, wait, just wait. Get off the porch! Let me try, I know her better than anyone. Let me try, I'll get her to realize who I am." They backed off the porch and I think they were glad to do so.

"Abby! Abby! Abby! It's me, Bear! Abby shut up! It's me, Bear!" I stood right in the front window. Knowing that on her wild run between windows she would eventually be here again. Oops! She looked, but was moving so fast I didn't think she saw me. So I yelled again. "Abby! It's me, Bear!" The blinds on the windows stopped swinging. The barking ceased. A couple of the blinds near the corner of the window parted. I knew Abby was standing in her chair by the door. Her funny, intense little face peered out at me with bewilderment and confusion. She fixed me with that marble streaked eye of hers and whispered my name, "Bear?" "Yes, it's me." "What on earth are you doing here?" "Abby, there are others with me. It's okay. Let us in." I heard the dead bolt click. I opened the door and went in followed by our team. Abby was still standing in the chair. The look on her face was total disbelief. The team was rather subdued by her solo performance. Queen and the others stayed in the yard.

"What's going on? Why are you guys here? Why aren't there any vehicles? Bear?" she looked pleadingly at me for an explanation. Before I could answer Buck said, "We've come to get you for Christmas Eve." Dakota piped up, "Everyone else was at Bill's and we thought you should be there too!"

Everyone said a few words about why we were there, but Smoky said it best. "Abby, we didn't want you to be alone on this very special night. Our good time was dimmed by your absence."

All the while we talked, the hair on the nap of Abby's neck didn't flatten and her tail remained tightly curled over her back. Her stiff-legged stance told me she hadn't dropped her guard. Slowly she looked at each of us and when her eyes met mine, she spoke directly to me. "Bear, is this true?" "Yes, Abby, it's true and you won't believe the story we have to tell you." She looked like she was melting. The hair went down and the tail relaxed. She slid slowly from the chair and took a couple of short steps. She dropped flat on her belly on the floor in our midst. She kept putting a front paw over her eye. Then she repeated the movement on the other side. I could have sworn she was crying. I'll bet a bag of my best treats that there wasn't a dry eye in the group. Even Ben and Deacon who were pretending to examine the Christmas tree didn't fool me. Abby quickly regained her composure and everyone began talking at once.

Over the din I heard Buddy say, "You'll ride on the sleigh with Misty and me." "Oh, no!" said Abby, "I can't go. I can't stand the cold anymore. The cold and freezing rain of that Iowa cornfield did something to my entire system. I appreciate your thoughts and all you've done, but I am afraid to spend that much time outside away from the house. I know that a simple "thank you", is hollow in the face of such daring and kindness, but that's all I can give. Please understand."

Buddy persisted, "Abby, you don't understand, we have wool blankets and a sheepskin to protect you. More than that, Abby, we have a miracle." "What do you mean, a miracle?" "Well, we may be good, but what has transpired tonight is far beyond any of our meager efforts."

I couldn't believe my ears. Buddy was actually admitting that what happened was not due to our efforts alone. I walked over to her and licked her head a couple of times. "Abby! Poor Abby! You'll be just fine with us. Don't worry. I promise."

The others began to regale Abby with stories of the trip down. I looked at them surrounding her with love and affection. I was proud of these dogs.

CHAPTER 20

I walked outside. Queen was sitting near the bottom step. "I've been waiting for you. I have a favor to ask." "I'll be happy to help you if I can. What's the favor?" "I couldn't believe the house when I saw it," she began, "little has changed!

The out buildings are newer and the pine trees and the bird feeders in the side yard are new. The apple trees are the same. The beautiful big porch, a good place to lay on a rainy day in summer. The houses across the street are gone but the other houses appear pretty much like they did fifty years ago. Here I go rattling on like an old lady. Back to my favor."

"Being a ghost or spirit has its limitations. One being freedom of movement. I know that sounds strange after just running the route with you folks, but take my word, it's complicated. What I would like is for you to accompany me on a short walk to a few of the old places I loved." "Oh, I'd be greatly honored," I said. "Where would you like to go?" "Just up the hill to Main Street and maybe over by the ball park. Is the park still there?" "Oh, yes. Give me a minute. I'll tell the others we won't be long. Would any of the other ahem...*ghosts* care to join us?" "No, we've already discussed it. King and Mister don't have very fond memories of town. They, along with Dingo, prefer to stay close to home and let the good times flow gently back."

I ran up on the porch and stuck my head in the front door, "Hey, guys. Queen and I are taking a little walk uptown. We won't be long."

As we started up the middle of the road I noticed Queen was studying the houses and buildings carefully. "Just here on my right stood a big old sprawling house. I had many a litter of pups under there." "What? Why?" "Well, it was private, warm and close to home. A wonderful couple lived there. They never complained until they would hear the puppies cry. Billy and the family would fix me the grandest birthing box anyone could wish for, but I preferred under that house."

"Right here under this street light and all around the Lutheran Church and yard we spent many glorious evenings. Children and dogs of all ages and sizes played together. Wonderful games of Kick the Can, Run My Good Sheep Run and Hide and Seek to name a few. Often, we dogs were scolded for inadvertently giving away hiding spots by standing and barking or just wagging our tails. What fun. Then as the evening wore on one by one parents would call the children home to bed. It was a great time to live."

As we crossed the street to the next block, Queen studied a tall dark house on the left. "Louie Coppick lived there. He raised hunting hounds and beagles. He saved my life oncc. I'd bccn poisoned and was dying—remember, this was in the day when people set poison out for rats and other pests—and Billy ran to get Louie. He came and forced some horrible concoction down my throat. It made me throw up. He worked over me quite some time. Vigorously rubbing my legs, belly and neck. He finally told Billy I've done all I can. Now we have to wait."

"I remember I couldn't move a muscle or make even the slightest sound. Billy covered me with blankets and sat next to me for hours and hours. Slowly I came back to the land of the living. It took me many weeks to gain back my strength and become my old self again."

We had reached Main Street and Queen looked first one way and then the next. "That's a fire hall. It's in the same place as it was before, but the building's different."
" I see the Swallow Inn is still in the same place," Queen said "and I'll venture its been there 100 years or more."
Queen turned and looked South down Main Street and

questioned what happened to the huge black smoke stack that marked Anderson's Lumber Mill. "Well", I replied, "I don't ever recall seeing a black smoke stack, but the Andersons still own a huge building supply company down here." We crossed the street and walked along side of the building. "Is that the park you're looking for?" I indicated an area to our right. "No, the one I mean is ahead and more to the left. I see, it's changed quite a bit. The fence around it use to be made of wood."

We had turned the corner and were walking along the chain link fence enclosing the ballpark. "Up ahead is the highway. One of Billy's best friends lived next to the building on the left. It was a garage in those days, looks like a store now. The boy had a dog named Tippy, a very good friend of mine."

"Hey, across the highway is the old school house. Do you want to go there?" "Oh no. I don't think so. That school is precisely why King wouldn't leave the yard tonight."

Normally, I'm not one to delve or pry, but I smelled something interesting. Queen's tone indicated there was a big story behind that statement. What was with the royal looking dog called King. If and when the opportunity arose, I would ask about him. We turned at the highway and headed west, walking parallel with it. "See that gray house directly across from us?" "Yes." "Well, that house is where the children's great aunts lived. What terrific ladies they were. You haven't lived unless you have heard "God Bless America" as sung by their Great Aunt Gert, as she madly clutched the steering wheel of her 1936 Chevy heading to a Sunday picnic. Their Great Aunt Phyl was the best cookie baker and stuffed toy maker in the entire world. Those women were fabulous." "Really? Chuck Parrett, a cousin of the children and his wife, Pat, own the house now." I added. I found it strange to use the word children about our folks.

We had reached the corner of Main Street and US-2. "Well for Heavens sake, it's Jack's Restaurant. I can't believe it! All these years. For all that has changed, it's really remarkable what has not." Queen stood on the corner looking around savoring the moment.

"I think we should start toward the house. We have to go back tonight." Queen indicated she heard me, but continued to gaze around the four corners of what had been her world. "Bear, don't fret about the trip back. If you were surprised and mystified by the trip down, you'll be absolutely astonished about the return trip." She looked like she might be ready to leave when I noticed she looked north toward the old school, her eyes looked sad. Finally she turned and headed south down Main Street toward home. We passed Bill's Bar. I was relieved. I felt we had to get started. There was so much to get organized before we left. We walked in silence to the end of the block, we turned right and started down the street where the Catholic Church is. Without stopping Queen started talking about King.

CHAPTER 21

"His story is the most tragic and heart breaking of any I have ever heard." She said. Everything about him was a mystery. How he came to town. Why he didn't like grown-ups. Why he wouldn't settle completely with one family and the reason for his death. Are all shrouded in mystery.

Many stories went around about when and how he got to town. One story said he had been stolen and escaped from his captors. Another story claimed he had been let out of a vehicle when it stopped in town and the owners couldn't find him or didn't realize that he was missing.

He was extremely shy around grown-ups. He avoided them at all costs. This of course made adults wary of him and they figured he wasn't to be trusted. King loved children and they in turn were crazy about him. He arrived in town in mid fall. A more majestic creature I have never seen, he was mammoth in dog size. King was totally white, long hair with a large bushy tail, a huge head with a kind looking face. I don't know why I am describing him, you have seen him. He took a fancy to my Billy. I must admit it bothered me a little when I would watch them roughhouse in the snow. However, I was the one who slept on the foot of Billy's bed each night. I never for a moment really felt left out. King spent the Christmas holidays with us. In fact, Christmas Eve was probably the only night he ever slept in the house or any house as far as that goes. Billy got a wonderful toy pump gun for Christmas and it shot small red plastic balls. Before Christmas morning, King had chewed each of the balls to the point where they would never work in the new gun. So much for that Christmas surprise. Maybe he was physic and had a reason to hate guns.

King was a true sled dog; he had been trained to pull. One day Billy and Chum Nelson hitched King up to a sleigh and the dog pulled them along the bay from Rapid River to Masonville. Chum's uncle had a boat rental on the bay. After a visit and a big meal for the boys and the dog, they decided to start back home. King refused to pull them back across the bay. He had a big lunch and was too full and lazy to work. Chum's uncle loaded the boys, the sled and King into his pickup and drove them back to Rapid River." Queen stopped in front of the Catholic Church and sat down. I did the same. She seemed pensive and lost in thought. "Are you okay?" I asked. "Is there anything I can do?" "No, it's just that I've never told the story of King's death before and it is more traumatic than I realized. It's a horrible story, but one that must be told once in awhile. If only to show how fear and ignorance blend together and destroy lives, hopes, dreams and sometimes childhood." I knew terrible things could happen, that's life. But whatever happened those many years ago at that school must have been really awful.

"It was late spring and the days were getting nice. There were still large patches of snow everywhere. Years ago most dogs ran free and, of course, they congregated where children played. A natural place for dogs to hang around was the schoolyard. Like I said, King didn't like adults and he remained aloof from them. This attitude made grown-ups uncomfortable. Certain teachers and parents didn't like the idea of this big dog hanging around. To my knowledge he never bit, growled or nipped at anyone. He was different and nobody knew anything about him. He didn't fit the mold of a proper town dog. One day, right after the noon bell rang and the children were settling in their classrooms, some shots rang out. The windows on the east side of the building were soon filled with horror stricken children. There on a patch of snow lay King. Standing over him with rifles were two policemen." "Dear Lord, you're not serious?" "Yes I am, unfortunately."

I could feel a big lump in my throat and I felt just awful. I couldn't believe what I had just heard. There were many unanswered questions racing through my head, but when I looked at Queen I couldn't bear to extend her pain. We sat quietly for a little while. Slowly we regained our composure. I couldn't help thinking how life gives us all such different roads to travel. There are many of us who always have the best. There are those who suffer greatly all their lives. Still others overcome tragedy, and though scared, struggle and make a good life. Then there are those who barely start to live when it's time to die.

It's true man has dominion over animals and we, as such, are for man's use. The catch to dominion is consideration and responsibility. As with all of nature, man is a caretaker. However, there are far too many men who are thoughtless, cruel, abusive and irresponsible. I believe that a day will come to all men when they will be asked about their role as caretakers of this spot in the universe. How did they care for the air, earth, water and animals, dumb or otherwise, two or four legged, webbed feet or winged?

I looked up at the night sky. The stars were brilliant against the velvet black of the night. I knew somewhere up there was a place for us. A place we could run and never tire. Where we would always be warm and well fed. Where a harsh word or hurtful blow would never come near. Where we would always be safe with our loved ones. I know my creator doesn't make throwaways.

Chapter 22

Queen's voice brought me back to the snow covered sidewalk, "Bear, it's time to go."

We walked down the alley to the back yard of the house and around to the front porch. I looked over to the side yard. The Shadow Team was still gathered around obviously enjoying this experience. I went up on the porch and yelled, "Time to go."

The door opened and out they tumbled. Abby in the midst and appearing most eager to get started. Queen had gone over to the Shadow Team and was talking with them. Misty, Abby and Buddy piled on the sleigh. Buddy was quiet, no longer the bossy little general, he was probably all talked out and just plain tired. The rest of the team stood in harness. I walked over to Queen to say good-bye. She met me by the corner of the porch. "Tabers has a request. He would like Buck to have an old toy of his." "Where is it? Is it in the house?" "No, Tabers said he buried it temporarily last spring when he was here. They left before he had time to dig it up." "Where is it?" "He said it's at the base of the old iron kettle in the back yard." "Okay, we'll get it. No problem."

I left the group and told Buck to follow me. We walked to the backyard and started sniffing and pawing around the old kettle. "Here it is!" "Gosh, it's Tabers old Boom Ba." "What's that?" Buck asked. "I don't know. I only know that's what they call it."

It was a hard rubber object that looked like one ball on top of another. I don't know why, but Tabers was absolutely goofy about it. Back in the front yard, Buck dropped the toy in the sleigh, we both harnessed up and stood ready to go. Queen walked over to us and nodded her approval. I looked and the Shadow Team was ready as well.

"Bear, and of course all of you other wonderful dogs, it had been our pleasure. Thank you for a truly fabulous evening. Perhaps someday we may join you in another adventure." Queen got in the sleigh and the Shadow

Team was ready. She called to us, "God be with you. Love to all." With that the teams were off across the road and onto the railroad grade. Heading north. Heading back. Heading home to our folks.

In a blur of tiny sparkling lights and the tinkling of small silver bells it was over. We were standing on the far edge of Bill's yard looking up at the house. We could see our people and hear music. I looked at our group. There stood Deacon and Ben each with a coil of rope. Buck had a bunch of belts. Shannon and Dakota each had a blanket. Smoky was carrying a sheepskin. Misty and Buddy each had a roll of tape. Abby had the "Boom Ba". I was carrying the snacks and some belts. I motioned and we started across the yard. Into the garage we went. We put everything away and headed into the laundry room, down the stairs, and into the den. If it hadn't been for Abby and Buck with the "Boom Ba", even I wouldn't have believed anything had happened.

CHAPTER 23

Christmas Eve was coming to a close and the folks were talking of leaving. The plans for Christmas Day were finalized and who was staying with whom was decided.

Peter was standing at the top of the stairs, "Hey! You guys let's let our four legged kids out once more before we leave." Mike joined him and started down the stairs followed by several others. Upon reaching the bottom of the stairs, Peter flipped the light on. Everyone stood

looking into the room. All that remained of the fire were a few glowing coals. The room was unearthly quiet considering the occupants and their natural ability to give loud and prolonged greetings.
"What the." "Who brought Abby?" "How'd she get here?" "Hey ! Who brought Abby?" Mike hollered up the stairs, "Lauren get down here."

Down the stairs bounced Lauren and stood by her Dad. "Lauren, did you sneak Abby in the car?" "No. I wouldn't do that." "Well, who did?" "Dad, I am serious. I wouldn't do it and everybody knows Abby doesn't do well in crowds."

Just then Peter remarked on the way the dogs were arranged around Abby, "Look! The dogs are sitting around her like they're protecting her or something. That's pretty wild."

Little Jake had come downstairs and had wiggled his way through the group. He started toward the dogs and they moved closer to Abby. Abby laid down and watched everyone. All of a sudden Jake spotted the toy that Buck had.

"Daddy, Daddy look. Buck's got Taber's Boom Ba." "What! Give me that. Where did this come from? Tabers lost that at Grandma's house in Rapid almost a year ago. What on earth is going on?"

Everyone began talking at once. More folks had come downstairs to see Abby. Old Mama came down and